BRITAIN'S BEST POLITICAL CART

Dr Tim Benson is Britain's leading authority on political cartoons. He runs the Political Cartoon Gallery and Café which is located near the River Thames in Putney. He has produced numerous books on the history of cartoons, including *David Low Censored*, *Giles's War*, *Churchill in Caricature*, *Low and the Dictators*, *The Cartoon Century: Modern Britain through the Eyes of its Cartoonists*, *Drawing the Curtain: The Cold War in Cartoons*, *Over the Top: A Cartoon History of Australia at War* and *How to be British: A Cartoon Celebration*.

Merry Christmas,
Dad!
Love Rach xxx

BRITAIN'S BEST POLITICAL CARTOONS 2023

Edited by Tim Benson

HUTCHINSON
HEINEMANN

1 3 5 7 9 10 8 6 4 2

Hutchinson Heinemann
20 Vauxhall Bridge Road
London SW1V 2SA

Hutchinson Heinemann is part of the Penguin
Random House group of companies whose addresses
can be found at global.penguinrandomhouse.com.

Penguin
Random House
UK

First published in the United Kingdom by Hutchinson Heinemann in 2023.

www.penguin.co.uk

A CIP catalogue record for this book is available from the British Library.

ISBN 9781529153873

Typeset in 9.75/14pt Amasis MT Pro by Jouve (UK), Milton Keynes
Printed and bound in Italy by L.E.G.O. S.p.A.

The authorised representative in the EEA is Penguin Random House Ireland,
Morrison Chambers, 32 Nassau Street, Dublin D02 YH68

Penguin Random House is committed to a sustainable future
for our business, our readers and our planet. This book is made
from Forest Stewardship Council® certified paper.

INTRODUCTION

Two stories have dominated the news agenda in 2023: the coronation of King Charles III and the continuing war in Ukraine. In last year's anthology I wrote about the monarchy. Sadly, a week after the book had gone to the printers, the Queen died. This year, eighteen months on from the launch of Vladimir Putin's invasion of Ukraine, I have decided to see what happens if I write about despots.

Monarchs and despots alike have attracted the attention of Britain's greatest cartoonists for two centuries or more but, whereas kings and queens have, for the most part, been treated with a fair degree of respect, tyrants have without exception been savaged. And they haven't liked it. Napoleon Bonaparte, Kaiser Wilhelm II, Benito Mussolini, Adolf Hitler – to name just a few – may have sought to present themselves as men of iron, but all proved to be thin-skinned, insecure, vainglorious ninnies when confronted by drawings that caricatured or ridiculed them. The same holds true today.

*

Napoleon Bonaparte was the first dictator to experience the pointy end of the political cartoonist's pen, when he was targeted by the father of the modern political cartoon, James Gillray. The French emperor regarded himself as a 'great man' of history. Gillray saw him rather differently, invariably depicting him as 'Little Boney', a vertically challenged upstart. This diminutive character first appeared in a cartoon of January 1803 – *German nonchalence* [*sic*] *- or - the vexation of little Boney* – but arguably achieved cartoon immortality in *Maniac-ravings - or - little Boney in a strong fit,* published just three months later, shortly after the breakdown of the Treaty of Amiens, which had briefly established peace between England and France. Here Little Boney is shown stamping his feet in a childish rage, cursing the British press and Parliament and threatening invasion – a broken globe at his feet symbolising the destructive force Gillray believed him to represent. As the threat the emperor posed to Britain grew ever greater, so in Gillray's cartoons he became ever smaller and more infantile: a child too big for his boots, weighed down by an increasingly oversized bicorn hat, enormous scabbard and immense spurs. Other British cartoonists followed suit, with Isaac Cruikshank, for example, starting to render Napoleon at half the height of his wife and troops.

Gillray's *Maniac-ravings - or - little Boney in a strong fit* (24 May 1803).

In reality, the victor of many battles stood at around 5 feet 7 inches tall – about par for men of his time. Thanks primarily to Gillray, however, the British public came to believe that the emperor really was as diminutive as the cartoonists made him out to be. It is thanks to their work that the label 'Napoleon complex' is now used to talk about the belief that short men seek to compensate for their lack of stature through aggressive behaviour.

Napoleon failed to see the funny side. According to the historian Frederick Kagan, he viewed such slighting depictions of him as a 'deliberate provocation', and even went so far as to send a flurry of diplomatic notes across the English Channel demanding that the British government censor Gillray's work. The cabinet, amused by his outrage, ignored him. Years later, when he was in exile on the isle of Elba, Napoleon was still smarting. He is supposed to have said that Gillray's depictions of him had been 'more damaging than a dozen generals', and that they had 'done more than all the armies of Europe to bring me down'. The image of Little Boney had done its work.

At the other end of the nineteenth century, Kaiser Wilhelm II of Germany also found himself the target of British cartoonists, and proved to be even more sensitive about the way he was treated than Napoleon had been. Not yet 30 when he assumed the throne in 1888, he was invariably portrayed as a childish, impulsive and somewhat ridiculous figure, with his waxed moustache and love of theatrical uniforms. His decision to dismiss Germany's long-standing senior statesman, Otto von Bismarck, in March 1890 prompted perhaps one of the most famous cartoons of all time: Sir John Tenniel's *Dropping the Pilot*, in which Bismarck is the elderly captain forced to disembark from his ship with the Kaiser idly looking on.

The Kaiser had a keen interest in political cartoons. Indeed, he was a long-term subscriber to *Punch,* which had been a staple of the Prussian royal palaces since the late 1850s, when Wilhelm's mother Victoria (eldest daughter of Queen Victoria of Great Britain) had married into the Prussian royal family. But there was only so much he could take. Matters came to a head in February 1892 when he gave an ill-advised, grandiose speech to the Brandenburg assembly in which he claimed to 'be on the path that Heaven has laid out for me'. Faced with a *Punch* cartoon by Edward Linley Sambourne, entitled *The Modern Alexander's Feast*, in which he was shown pompously toasting himself on the clouds of Mount Olympus, he wrote to his grandmother, Queen Victoria, seeking to persuade her to stop publication of the magazine. She explained that such a move was not 'quite within [my] province', although she did say that she was prepared to make it known to the magazine's editor that critical cartoons of her grandson were damaging Anglo-German relations. *Punch* responded by publishing *Wilful Wilhelm* by Sambourne on 26 March 1892, which shows a childlike Kaiser angrily tearing at his copy of *Punch* with a smashed copy of *Dropping the*

Pilot in the background. Amid the broken furniture around him is a broken globe – seemingly a nod to Gillray's cartoon of 'Little Boney'. The verse that accompanies the cartoon tauntingly reads: 'My Wilful Wilhelm, you'll not win / By dint of mere despotic din; / By kicking everybody over / In whom a critic you discover / Or shouting in your furious way, / "Oh! Take the nasty *Punch* away!"'

Sambourne's *Wilful Wilhelm* (26 March 1892).

Within Germany the Kaiser could launch prosecutions of critical journalists for offences against the dignity of the sovereign (prosecutions against the press reached a high in Germany in the early 1890s). Faced with mockery from across the North Sea, the best he could do was to cancel his subscription to *Punch*. By 1904 he was also making sure that unflattering depictions of him were removed from any copies of the magazine that reached the German border.

The constant trickle of anti-Kaiser cartoons turned into a flood when Britain declared war against Germany in 1914. Now he became the embodiment of the wicked Hun, depicted as either a monster or a farcical tyrant. In his anthology of his cartoons for the *Daily Express*, entitled *The Kaiser's Kalendar for 1915 – Or the Dizzy Dream of Demented Willie*, Sidney Strube opted for the latter approach. Here 'Little Willie' happily dreams of dressing up as a Roman soldier and conquering London, his sausage dog in tow. In June *I Personally Conduct My Own Opera at Covent Garden*. In October *I Play the 'Loot' over the Ruins of the Bank of England*. Safely ensconced on the English side of the North Sea, Strube could do what he liked. Acutely aware, though, that the Kaiser's reach extended to much of continental Europe, the *Express* thought it as well to print a warning on the back of the anthology: '*The Daily Express* warns purchasers not to send these Calendars to Troops at the Front, as the Germans have been known to inflict punishment on prisoners on whom they have found caricatures of the Kaiser.'

It wasn't just British soldiers who were threatened; Wilhelm sought to menace the cartoonists, too. In June 1915 the German daily newspaper *Deutsche Tageszeitung* was instructed by the Kaiser to issue a warning to those cartoonists who drew for *Punch* that 'when the day of reckoning arrives we shall know with whom we have to deal and how to deal with them.' *Punch*'s response, later that month, was to published a cartoon by Leonard Raven-Hill entitled *On the Black List*, showing Mr Punch and Kaiser Wilhelm struggling over a hangman's noose. As the Kaiser loses his grip, Mr Punch threatens him with his

The Kaiser signing the death-warrant of certain English cartoonists.

Alfred Leete's response to the Kaiser's threat, entitled *The Kaiser signing the death-warrant of certain English cartoonists*, published in the *London Opinion* of 26 June 1915.

spear-like pen. The caption reads: 'Kaiser: "I'm going to hang you." / Punch: "Oh, you are, are you? Well, you don't seem to know how the scene ends. It's the hangman that gets hanged."'

That the Kaiser was in deadly earnest when he made his threats is demonstrated by the fate of the Dutch cartoonist Louis Raemaekers, whose work was regularly published in the Amsterdam *Telegraaf*. The Dutch authorities were sufficiently worried by his anti-Kaiser stance as to confiscate his work on occasion when they thought he had overstepped the mark, their fear being that the notoriously sensitive German leader might be so outraged that he would order an attack on neutral Holland. For his part, the Kaiser so hated Raemaekers' tendency to portray him as an ally of Satan that he got his government to put relentless pressure on the Dutch minister of foreign affairs to stop the errant cartoonist from drawing 'anything that tends towards insulting the German Kaiser and the German army'. Raemaekers was eventually arrested for 'endangering Holland's neutrality'. When he was acquitted, the Kaiser put a bounty of 12,000 guilders on his head and anonymous death threats against his wife were made. In 1916, Raemaekers and his family fled to England. Here they were welcomed with open arms by British politicians and journalists, and Raemaekers embarked on a new career as cartoonist for newspapers such as the *Daily Mail* and *The Times*. British Prime Minister David Lloyd George was so impressed by his work that he persuaded him to tour the United States to drum up support for Britain and her allies. Henry Perry Robinson, who reported for *The Times*, later claimed that Raemaekers was one of six people – including statesmen and military leaders – who had a decisive influence on the outcome of the war. Theodore Roosevelt, former president of the United

A propaganda poster by Louis Raemaekers showing Uncle Sam, the symbol of the US government, squaring up to a German butcher wearing a soldier's helmet and blood-soaked apron.

States, even said that Raemaekers' 'cartoons constitute the most powerful contribution made by neutrals to the cause of civilization in the World War'.

The fascist dictators who came to power in the following decades were as unamused by those who lampooned them as Napoleon and the Kaiser had been. Benito Mussolini, who had worked as a journalist and newspaper editor before he became the leader of Italy in 1922, regularly banned foreign publications and cartoonists that he felt treated him with insufficient respect and went so far as to refer to the *Daily Dispatch* cartoonist, George Butterworth, as a 'dangerous enemy'. Arguably, he loathed the great David Low even more, banning sales in Italy of both the *Evening Standard* and the *Manchester Guardian* in the wake of the 1935 publication of a Low cartoon showing the Italian dictator being waved off to war in Abyssinia by Hitler, Joseph Goebbels and Hermann Goering, all dressed as women (*The Girls He Left Behind Him*) against a backdrop dominated by a gravestone on which appear the words 'To the Abyssinian gamble – via Adowa?' – a taunting reference to the great Italian defeat at Adowa in the First Italo-Ethiopian War of 1896.

Thereafter, David Low's cartoons were never shown in the Italian press, except on the occasions when they were held up for mockery. His *Suezcide?* for example, which shows Mussolini in Roman armour shivering as he tests the temperature of the Suez Canal with his big toe, was reproduced in the Roman newspaper *Il Tevere*, alongside its own cartoon of John Bull, the personification of the British common man, floundering in the waters of the canal. The banner caption reads: 'Our answer to the degraded Low of the *Evening Standard*.' (Interestingly, the Nazis adopted a similar approach to cartoons critical of them. Hitler's foreign press secretary, Harvard-educated Ernst 'Putzi' Hanfstaengl, was the genius behind an unusual and very successful book, *Hitler in der Karikatur der Welt / Tat gegen Tinte* [Hitler in the World's Cartoons / Facts versus Ink], which turned critical cartoons back on the cartoonists by pointing out 'errors' in their assumptions.)

David Low's *Suezcide?* published in the *Evening Standard* on 16 September 1935.

One regular feature of Low's cartoons proved a particular irritant for Mussolini: a dog Low elected to call 'Musso'. Eventually, an official at the Italian embassy in London was ordered to contact the cartoonist in order to convey 'the regrets of the entire Italian people at the desecration of this exalted surname'. The official (described by Low as 'excited') then 'requested – nay, demanded – that in the interests of international concord the dog be rechristened'. Low affected to be astonished. There were, he informed the diplomat, probably 500 Mussolinis in the Rome telephone book and certainly two in London. It was a coincidence that Il Duce and his dog happened to share the same name. And if the official was seriously suggesting that Musso should be renamed, then what should be done about dogs bearing names of other celebrated Romans, such as Caesar and Nero?

Rather surprisingly, Mussolini's German counterpart, Adolf Hitler (himself an artist of sorts), started out as a David Low fan (he even requested a couple of originals from the cartoonist, although nothing came of it). But this was because he wrongly assumed that anyone who lampooned British politicians as regularly as Low did must be opposed to the system those politicians represented. Once he was in power, however, Hitler's attitude to cartoonists in general, and Low in particular, swiftly changed. He loathed a cartoon Sidney Strube produced during the Berlin Olympics in 1936 so much that he had all that day's copies of the *Daily Express* confiscated on arrival in Germany. On another occasion in November 1938, the German legation in Luxembourg brought a case against a left-wing magazine, *Escher Tageblatt*, and its editor, Hubert-Clément, for publishing a cartoon that showed the Führer in 'a state of violent exacerbation while making a speech'. Clément insisted that he had no intention of insulting Hitler and, when the Germans realised that the publicity surrounding the case threatened to make the cartoon universally known, they let the case drop.

Cecil Orr's cartoon for the *Daily Record* (1 December 1938) comments on the German government's lawsuit against the *Escher Tageblatt*.

Thereafter, the leaders of the Nazi regime adopted much the same approach to criticism as the Kaiser had done: they claimed that it was damaging Anglo-German relations. Germany's minister of propaganda, Joseph Goebbels, said as much to Britain's foreign secretary, Lord Halifax, in 1937 when he explained just how sensitive Hitler was to criticism in the British press (he singled out David Low, in particular). At the end of the meeting Halifax promised that 'the Government would do everything in its power to induce the London Press to avoid unnecessary offence' and, once back in England, duly got in touch with those newspapers whose cartoonists were causing trouble. As he confirmed in a letter to the then British ambassador in Berlin, Sir Nevile Henderson: 'I am hoping to see the *Daily Herald* and *Daily News* controlling powers myself.' He conceded, however, that 'I haven't as yet devised any approach that is satisfactory to Low, who draws the pictures in the *Evening Standard*, and these I expect are the most troublesome of any.' In the end, the foreign secretary decided to make a direct approach to the *Evening Standard*'s manager, Mike Wardell, and ask him if he could get Low to restrain himself a bit. 'You cannot imagine the frenzy that these cartoons cause,' he said. 'As soon as a copy of the *Evening Standard* arrives, it is pounced on for Low's cartoon and, if it is of Hitler, as it generally is, telephones buzz, tempers rise, fevers mount, and the whole governmental system of Germany is in uproar. It has hardly subsided before the next one arrives.'

Wardell's response was to say that he could not control Low even if he wanted to, nor could Lord Beaverbrook, the proprietor of the *Evening Standard*. Low's contract gave him complete creative control over his cartoons, and the newspaper could refuse to publish them only if they were obscene or libellous. Wardell went on to suggest that Halifax might be more effective if he were to talk to Low face to face. Halifax agreed and the meeting with the cartoonist took place. Low later described how the conversation went:

Once a week Hitler had my cartoons brought out and laid on his desk in front of him, and he finished always with an explosion. That he was extremely sore; his vanity was badly touched. He really bit the carpet . . . So the Foreign Secretary asked me to modify my criticism, in order that a better chance could be had for making friendly relations. I didn't want to start World War II. I said that I thought it was my duty, as a pressman, to speak the truth and I think this man's awful, but in view of the situation, I would be good.

'And so I was good,' he concluded, 'for about three weeks. Then Hitler walked into Austria.'

After Germany invaded Poland in 1939, the gloves came off on both sides. British cartoonists became more savage. The Nazis became more threatening. When, in December 1939, three months after the Second World War had broken out, Philip Zec drew a cartoon for the *Daily Mirror* showing an isolated Hitler eating Christmas dinner alone, the response from Berlin was not a diplomatic protest but a death threat. As Zec recalled: 'Some days later, we were sent a copy of a German newspaper in which they described me as "this filthy lying hyena scum". The article went on to say that amongst the first dozen people to be shot when the Germans arrived in London would be me.' After the war Zec, along with Low, Leslie Illingworth and just about every Fleet Street cartoonist, discovered that their names featured in the Nazi Black Book – a secret list, produced by the SS, of the people to be immediately arrested if Germany invaded Britain.

Given that Goebbels once observed that 'a joke ceases to be a joke when it relates to the Nazi regime and its leaders,' it is hard to conceive of any cartoon that would not have caused offence in Germany – nor in Italy where, according to Low, an official once told him: 'If we allowed the cartoonist any licence here, he would be making jokes about Fascism, and that would never do.' The British sense of humour didn't exactly help: quite simply, European fascist leaders were bewildered by it. Sidney Strube argued that they couldn't understand how, '[a]s they goose-stepped along to their downfall, we in this country laughed our way through our difficulties. The flooded air raid shelter, the snorer, the shelter bore, "my bomb story", spam, sand in the desert and mud in Italy, all these things cartoonists turned to a smile,' he went on. He also observed that the 'Nazis couldn't laugh at themselves, and at the end they were afraid to laugh at all.' Hitler once instructed Joseph Goebbels and his psychiatrists to study a Bruce Bairnsfather First World War cartoon to establish what made the British laugh, the cartoon in question being the famous one of a couple of Tommies standing in a shell-hole with one saying to the other: 'Well, if you knows of a better 'ole, go to it'. The sardonic tone of the cartoon was completely lost on Goebbels, who informed the Führer that the gag revolved around the fact that '[t]he soldier is standing in a big shell-hole . . . and what he means is that this is a German shell-hole and that we make the biggest shell-holes in the world.'

'WELL, IF YOU KNOWS OF A BETTER 'OLE, GO TO IT.'

Bruce Bairnsfather's famous First World War cartoon was published in the Christmas issue of the *Bystander*, on 24 November 1915.

That cartoonists are so good at getting under the skin of despots should come as no surprise. Tyrants desperately want to be taken seriously. Cartoonists refuse to oblige. 'I have learned from experience,' wrote David Low, 'that, in the bluff and counterbluff of world politics, to draw a hostile war lord as a horrible monster is to play his game. What he doesn't like is being shown as a silly ass.' In much

the same way, Steve Bell, cartoonist for the *Guardian*, has observed that the role of the political cartoonist is akin to the little boy in the story 'The Emperor's New Clothes': 'We're the ones that point and say, "Look! He hasn't got any clothes on!" Somebody has to point out sometimes that this is a lot of nonsense. The cartoonist does that and makes everybody laugh. That's the one thing totalitarians, tyrants and despots of all types cannot stand.'

David Low's *The Scourge of Mankind* illustrates his belief that drawing despots as asses rather than tyrants is far more effective at grating on their nerves.

Today's cartoonists draw on many of the same ridiculing techniques as their forebears did. They mock despots' physiques. They laugh at their egos. When it comes to portraying Vladimir Putin, for

Brian Adcock imagines Putin's invitation to potential international allies in his cartoon for the *Independent* on 5 April 2022.

This *Evening Standard* cartoon by Christian Adams (14 November 2022) plays on Putin's diminutive height to comment on Russia's awkward diplomatic position following talks between Joe Biden and Xi Jinping at the G20 summit.

example, many cartoonists follow in Gillray's footsteps by zeroing in on his perceived lack of inches. Peter Brookes of *The Times* says that he enjoys 'demeaning [Putin] by [reference to] his short stature'. Patrick Blower of the *Daily Telegraph* asserts that harping on about Putin's lack of height 'offers the constant chance to depict him as simultaneously macho man and weakling'. Kevin Kallaugher mocks Putin's stature and also the aggression he believes lurks in Putin's facial features: 'Putin has a funky stubby nose leading to an angry little mouth. The key to any caricature of Putin is his angry KGB eyes.' Christian Adams of the *Evening Standard*, meanwhile,

likes to subvert Putin's testosterone-fuelled persona by drawing him with a pot belly in the hope that it would upset him if he were to see it. *Independent* cartoonist Brian Adcock seeks to humiliate him, too: 'Putin has such a deluded sense of self, he's a complete narcissist. He thinks he's such a tough guy riding bare chested on horseback. It is so much fun to poke fun at that. I like to try and humiliate him as much as possible, prick that ridiculous ego. I like to draw him with flabby man-boobs and really long nipples. He doesn't have long nipples but I just like to draw him that way as I think if he ever saw it, it would really annoy him.'

Tyrants' lack of anything approaching nuance is also a gift for cartoonists. According to Rebecca Hendin, cartoonist for the *Guardian* and *New Statesman*, 'All cartoonists relish drawing despots, as they are generally ready-made cartoon characters, dealing in absolutes, in black and white and leave little need for exaggeration.' Brian Adcock looks forward to drawing despots because he gets 'to draw and comment on the most hideous people on the planet, a chance to expose them to the world'. Steve Bright of the *Sun* believes cartoonists enjoy drawing despots in the same way actors like playing baddies: 'They're so much more fun to take on, and cathartic to draw.'

Other contemporary authoritarian leaders receive similar treatment. Xi Jinping of China is regularly depicted by Peter Brookes as having ridiculous hair. For Andy Davey 'the stream of implausible Stalinist lunatics that North Korea provides, especially the mad haircuts' provides the same level of inspiration. Christian Adams further notes that Kim Jong-un is 'very, very short' and depicts him thus in the hope that 'he would hate that'.

Whether or not the former leader of the Free World can be described as a would-be despot is a matter of debate, but it is worth noting that cartoonists have treated Donald Trump much as they have treated the Putins, Xis and Kims of this world. Pocket cartoonist Nick Newman believes that, 'as a purely comic despot, Trump has to be my favourite, because his despotism, or attempts at despotism if that's what you'd call it, failed.' Henny Beaumont (cartoonist for the *Guardian*) argues that 'You can have such fun with his ridiculous yellow hair, orange skin and pouty mouth. It amused me to draw his long red tie as a snake and when he was defeated, I drew him as a big orange puddle.' Rebecca Hendin also has a soft spot for Trump, but for a rather different reason: 'He's easy to draw and I'm a sucker for an easy drawing.'

As a rule, even extreme savaging of the more autocratic of today's world leaders causes little controversy. As Peter Brookes puts it: 'There is no opposition to your depiction of a despot as everyone tends to agree with you.' According to Andy Davy, 'They're an easy target. I often feel a little like a cop-out when drawing them because they are such universal hate-figures and nobody is going to disagree with my ridiculing of them.' Patrick Blower concurs: 'Tyrants are unambiguous "baddies", which is always useful for cartoonists.' This lack of ambiguity can create problems for pocket cartoonists, though. Pockets are, in essence, topical gags that are supposed to be jovial and, as we know, dictators committing genocide is not exactly a laugh a minute. According to Nick Newman, 'With despotism comes all the things you don't want to think about, human rights abuses, war crimes etc., which make jokes for the pocket cartoonist well-nigh impossible. To be honest I'd rather despots didn't exist.' Steve Bell expresses a slightly different reservation, warning that cartoonists 'should not trivialise despots by harping on about goodies and baddies and that "evil" Putin is responsible for all that is bad in the world'.

Nick Newman's pocket cartoon for *The Times* (5 December 2022) was published following the news that two critics of President Putin had been found dead after falling from hotel windows.

Today's authoritarian leaders are as unforgiving of mockery and criticism as those who came before them. As Steve Bright puts it: 'I suspect you have to be fairly humourless to be an effective despot, and I imagine that being laughed at really gets up their despotic noses.' Lampoons by non-native cartoonists may no longer cause the diplomatic incidents they once did (Peter Brookes for one believes that, 'unlike previous dictators, [Putin] doesn't seem to give a damn'), but local critics are rarely tolerated.

Mikhail Zlatkovsky offers a case in point. A leading Moscow cartoonist, he was allowed, early in his career, to draw Gorbachev and then Yeltsin (he had also drawn Stalin, although the cartoon that he drew of him as a teenager in 1959 was not published until 1988). When Putin was Yeltsin's deputy, Zlatkovsky also drew him. However, the day after Putin's inauguration in May 2000, Zlatkovsky's editor came to see him after a visit to the Kremlin: 'He said to me, "Misha, we're not going to draw Putin anymore. The young lad is very sensitive," ' recalled Zlatkovsky. From that day onwards, he, along with other Russian cartoonists, found it impossible to get a cartoon of Putin published unless it presented the leader in a heroic light. And as Putin gained a firmer grip on power, the number of taboo subjects increased: according to Zlatkovsky, ministers, Kremlin aides and top military brass all became off limits. One *Guardian* cartoonist told me that when he was in Moscow in 2016 on a British Council trip, his minder repeatedly told him to stop drawing cartoons of Putin on restaurant napkins lest it should catch the attention of eagle-eyed officials. These days, being a political cartoonist in Putin's Russia means being a propagandist for the regime. Caricaturing Putin is forbidden and carries ever more significant risks; after Russia's invasion of Ukraine it was ruled that cartoonists who produced the 'wrong' sort of cartoons could be found guilty of spreading 'fake news' and face up to 15 years in prison.

The fact that despots continue to be fearful of cartoons that mock them shows how important it is that they should still be drawn. Brian Adcock believes satire remains one of the best ways to get to an autocrat: 'Laughing at the powerful, especially despots, is a brilliant way to try and bring them down to size.' Nicola Jennings of the *Guardian* thinks satirising despots may make them a figure of fun but in doing so 'it criticises their behaviour'. Andy Davey agrees that cartoons have a serious purpose, while also bringing much-needed relief to seriously depressing news: 'I don't think it trivialises their actions – well, no more than cartoons trivialise everything by the mildly humorous ("Horatian") satirical style that dominates newspaper cartoons. I guess such tyrants deserve a colder, harder "Juvenalian" treatment but readers get fed up with serious stuff and look to the cartoon for some relief.'

This year's edition of *Britain's Best Political Cartoons* proves that Patrick Blower was correct when he said that 'the great privilege of living in a liberal democracy is that we can not only openly mock our own leaders but that of other nations too. When occasion demands, cartoonists can jettison the jokes to produce powerful visual commentary on the actions and crimes of tyrants.' British cartoonists are, and have always been, unsurpassed when it comes to confronting and ridiculing despots. Of course, we all wish we could live in peace and harmony with benign political leaders who have their populace's best interests at heart. Unfortunately this is often not the case. And so our finest practitioners will continue belittling these despotic tyrants who have metaphorical and often literal 'blood on their hands'. As Rebecca Hendin says: 'Life would be better with no despots. I'd rather draw a utopia filled with cats. But as long as despots are despoting, it seems like a good idea to draw them.'

THE CARTOONS

With the votes of Conservative Party members being tallied, all the signs were that Liz Truss would succeed Boris Johnson as the next party leader and therefore the UK's new prime minister. This was confirmed when the results were announced (5 September), showing that Truss had gained 57.4 per cent of votes compared to her rival Rishi Sunak's 42.6 per cent. While Sunak had been critical of Johnson's time at the helm, Truss had been comparatively generous – and was rumoured to be Johnson's preferred choice. One of the odder incidents of Johnson's leadership had been his retreat into a refrigeration unit during the 2019 general election campaign, evading reporters' questions.

3 September 2022
Ben Jennings
Independent

On 2 September, the Russian state energy company Gazprom expanded its shutdown of the major Nord Stream 1 gas pipeline into western Europe. Gazprom justified the move as the result of technical issues with turbines; but it was widely seen as yet more politically motivated weaponisation of energy supplies by Vladimir Putin, targeting Western backers of Ukraine, notably Germany. In February 2022, in retaliation for the Russian invasion of Ukraine, Germany had refused certification for the newly built Nord Stream 2 pipeline, which now appeared to be a white elephant.

5 September 2022
Nicola Jennings
Guardian

Liz Truss was officially asked to form a government as Britain's 56th prime minister after her audience with Queen Elizabeth on 6 September. The meeting took place at the royal Balmoral estate, not long after Boris Johnson had visited to tend, formally, his resignation. According to the cartoonist, 'This particular moment when a new prime minister meets the monarch is called "the kissing of hands". Liz Truss was acting as though everything she did was right, everyone else was wrong, and she [Liz] wouldn't listen. So, it was almost as if the Queen was expected to kiss her hand, rather than the other way around.'

7 September 2022
Peter Brookes
The Times

On 8 September, the Second Elizabethan Age came to an end with the death of Queen Elizabeth II at Balmoral, at the age of ninety-six. Reigning for 70 years, she was the longest-serving monarch in British history. Her son, the new King Charles III, said: 'We mourn profoundly the passing of a cherished sovereign and a much-loved mother.' Four months before her death, on 17 May, the Queen had attended the opening of the Elizabeth line, a new railway running from the west to the east of London, named in her honour.

9 September 2022
Ben Jennings
Guardian

10 September 2022
Steve Bright
Sun

The Queen's passing came just 17 months after that of her husband Prince Philip, the Duke of Edinburgh. Winston Churchill had been prime minister when she acceded to the throne, and she went on to appoint 14 further prime ministers over her reign, most recently Liz Truss. She held weekly audiences with her prime minister throughout her reign.

Between 14 and 19 September, the body of Queen Elizabeth II lay in state in Westminster Hall, guarded by members of the Household Cavalry, the Foot Guards and the Sovereign's Bodyguard. Vast numbers of the public waited many hours to see the late monarch, creating a queue that snaked around London's streets for more than five miles. The cartoon deliberately evokes the Saatchi & Saatchi-designed Conservative poster for the 1979 general election, which was issued at a time of industrial strife and ran with the slogan 'Labour isn't working'.

13 September 2022
Patrick Blower
Daily Telegraph

16 September 2022
Steve Bell
Guardian

Liz Truss was due to meet the new King Charles III, as plans were finalised for the late Queen's funeral. At the same time, 'sources close to' the new chancellor, Kwasi Kwarteng, let it be known that he was considering scrapping regulations that capped bankers' bonuses. Introduced in the wake of the 2008 financial crash, these rules restricted bonuses to twice the amount of an individual's salary. Abolishing them would, it was hoped, unleash the City of London's strength against other world financial centres. The cartoonist heard the sound of champagne corks popping for the nation's fat cats.

In a televised address on 21 September, Russian President Vladimir Putin announced a partial mobilisation to prosecute the war against Ukraine. Putin justified the call up as a response to Western ambitions to 'destroy our country'. He also spoke darkly, if vaguely, of Russia's 'many weapons' which, he said, were better than NATO's. And he insisted that he was not bluffing about Russia using 'all the means' at its disposal if necessary – a clear reference to potential use of nuclear weapons. To some observers, it appeared that Putin's grip on reality was slipping further away.

22 September 2022
Dave Brown
Independent

As anticipation of the end to bankers' bonus caps grew, Liz Truss flew to the United States. Addressing businesspeople in New York, she said she wanted 'the City [of London] to be the most competitive place for financial services in the world', insisting that 'when we unblock capital' it would 'make every industry become more productive and competitive', becoming 'a key part of the levelling-up agenda'. In the Disney animated film *Peter Pan* (1953), Peter and his friends take to the skies to the refrain 'We Can Fly! We Can Fly! We Can Fly!', as they seek the faraway and fantastical 'Neverland'.

22 September 2022
Steve Bell
Guardian

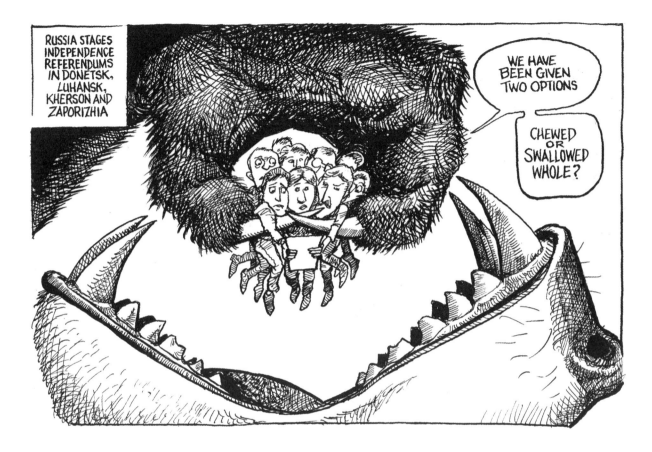

From 23 September, Russian occupying authorities in the Donetsk, Luhansk, Zaporizhzhia and Kherson regions of eastern Ukraine began conducting referenda on joining the Russian Federation. The Russian foreign ministry subsequently declared that 'people were not afraid to come to the polls and express their will' and claimed that up to 99.23 per cent of voters approved unification with Russia, in turnouts as high as 97.5 per cent. However, G7 leaders and other international critics saw the referenda as illegitimate shams, and the Ukrainian media spoke of voters forced to go to the polls at gunpoint, in areas that had been partially depopulated anyway.

25 September 2022
Kevin Kallaugher
Economist

25 September 2022
Chris Riddell
Observer

On 23 September, in a dramatic statement soon dubbed the 'mini budget', Kwasi Kwarteng announced a series of eye-catching tax cuts, including abolition of the higher rate (45 per cent) of income tax. 'For too long in this country,' he declaimed, 'we have indulged in a fight over redistribution. Now, we need to focus on growth.' Given the scale of the borrowing needed to pay for both the tax cuts and the Truss government's spending on home energy subsidies – estimated at £45 billion – it appeared to be a high-risk strategy, especially as the chancellor had forgone the usual forecasts from the Office of Budget Responsibility.

Some commentators, newspapers and the head of the Confederation of British Industry immediately lauded the growth agenda of the Kwarteng mini budget. By contrast, it did not take long for international markets and others, from the Labour Party to the International Monetary Fund, to deliver a different verdict. The pound quickly fell steeply against other currencies, almost reaching parity with the US dollar. To try and calm jitters, the Treasury announced that the Office of Budget Responsibility would, after all, provide some due diligence by way of an economic forecast on the impact of the mini budget.

26 September 2022
Christian Adams
Evening Standard

26 September 2022
Nicola Jennings
Guardian

Vladimir Putin's call-up of reservists and those with military experience to fight in Ukraine was the first mobilisation of Russian society since the Second World War, when the homeland had been under attack. Around Russia, there were now reports of anti-war and anti-call-up protests breaking out; and some Russians liable to serve were seeking a quick exit from the country, flooding over the border into Finland or catching one-way flights to foreign destinations. The cartoonist refashions the familiar 1914 recruitment image featuring Lord Kitchener.

For more than a week, Iran had been gripped by protests against the clerical regime's strict laws, and especially against its Morality Police. The spark was the death, in police custody, of the 22-year-old Jina 'Mahsa' Amini on 16 September, after she was arrested for wearing her hijab (headscarf) incorrectly. In response, women and girl protestors threw off their hijabs, cut their hair and took to the streets, shouting their slogan 'Women, Life, Freedom!' They were joined by many others disaffected with the Iranian regime, and supported beyond Iran by a huge cast, from Hollywood celebrities to civil rights groups.

26 September 2022
Morten Morland
The Times

KAMIKWASI...

BANZAI!!

HMS BRITANNIA

30 September 2022
Dave Brown
Independent

To critics of the mini budget, it looked as though the prime minister and her chancellor were on course to sink the UK economy. Holders of UK debt rushed to sell it off, the Bank of England stepped in to forestall damage to pension funds, while mortgage lenders withdrew hundreds of products amid rising interest rates, and the International Monetary Fund said the mini budget would increase inequality. In awkward regional radio interviews, Truss tried to defend the measures, blaming global factors. Shadow Chancellor Rachel Reeves wanted Parliament recalled, 'so this kamikaze budget can be reversed'.

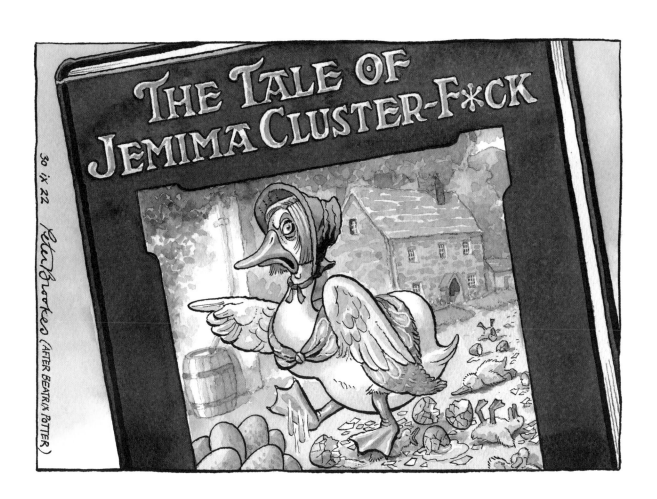

By the end of September, Truss's prime ministership was swallowed up by the turbulence following the mini budget. According to the cartoonist, 'I drew this cartoon in a state of complete despair at how everything Liz Truss touched turned to dross. She'd basically trashed the Tory Party, so here I show her smashing her eggs and crushing her own. I like Beatrix Potter as a vehicle, because what you're doing with it politically is in complete contrast to the tame drawing style. And you wouldn't expect an asterisked Beatrix Potter title.'

30 September 2022
Peter Brookes
The Times

By the beginning of October, almost half of mortgage products from lenders had disappeared from the market since the mini budget, while a raised price cap looked set to increase average home energy costs to £2,500 per annum – costs that would have been higher still without the subsidy of the new Energy Price Guarantee. As the cartoonist put it, 'Mortgage holders faced a ticking time bomb as surging interest rates outstripped energy bills as the financial crisis deepened. It's hard to know, amid the pervasive smell of cordite in the Truss–Kwarteng ascendancy, which bomb was the most dangerous.'

1 October 2022
Andy Davey
Daily Telegraph

On 30 September, Vladimir Putin declared that Luhansk, Donetsk, Zaporizhzhia and Kherson were formally new regions (*oblasts*) of the Russian Federation. According to the cartoonist, 'When Putin signed the treaties for the formal annexation of parts of Ukraine, I did him using red blood instead of ink. I've used our old friend, the leaky pen from King Charles's Pengate cartoon, with the actual words the King used.' Video footage of King Charles deprecating his leaking fountain pen went viral in September.

1 October 2022
Peter Brookes
The Times

3 October 2022
Christian Adams
Evening Standard

In the febrile political and economic climate, the Conservative Party Conference got under way in Birmingham, and on 2 October Kwasi Kwarteng faced his party's restive MPs and activists. His big speech had been trailed as a bullish determination to outface the critics and 'stay the course' with the mini budget policies. In the event, and under pressure, Kwarteng executed a last-minute U-turn on the measure whose optics had been proving so damaging for the government and Conservative Party: the removal of the 45-pence higher rate of income tax. It would, instead, stay.

GETTING BEHIND LIZ

10.10.22 DAVID SIMONDS

Despite attempts to rally the Conservative Party troops at the Birmingham conference, an air of rebellion still hung over the Tory backbenches. Several figures, including Boris Johnson, called on Conservatives to get behind Liz Truss, or possibly face oblivion at the next general election. But backbench rebels, said to number at least thirty, were convinced that they could chip away at further elements of the mini budget, such as cuts to welfare, given that a U-turn on the 45-pence tax rate had already been extracted.

10 October 2022
David Simonds
Evening Standard

11 October 2022
Christian Adams
Evening Standard

Continuing volatility in the market for UK gilts (bonds) prompted yet more intervention by the Bank of England, 'against the backdrop of an unprecedented repricing in UK assets'. On 28 September the Bank had announced it stood 'ready to restore market functioning and reduce any risks from contagion to credit conditions for UK households and businesses'. The impression that the Bank was trying to clear up the mess caused by the mini budget only intensified.

A spokesman for Liz Truss denied that she thought her colleague Michael Gove was a 'sadist', after so-called 'friends of the prime minister' had described him so, adding that he had a 'corrupted soul' and 'a darkness inside him'. The *Mail on Sunday* reported that, at the party conference, Truss had discussed appointing Gove as an ambassador – before he publicly rubbished the plan to axe the 45-pence tax rate, saying it displayed the 'wrong values'. Number 10's denials coincided with the launch of a reported charm offensive to win over Conservative backbenchers. (The cartoon evokes children's war comics of an earlier era.)

11 October 2022
Steve Bell
Guardian

As economic woes mounted, 'there wasn't', according to the cartoonist, 'much longer left for Kwarteng as chancellor. Quasimodo [the despairing hero of Victor Hugo's *The Hunchback of Notre-*Dame] said "The bells, the bells" so here that became "The bills, the bills", because mortgage rate rises were causing massive problems. The idea to use Quasimodo in this sort of context was actually sent to me by a reader. This very rarely happens, but if you're lucky and they send you one like this that works, that's great.'

12 October 2022
Peter Brookes
The Times

When King Charles held an audience with his new prime minister, Liz Truss, on 13 October, he welcomed her with the question 'Back again?', before exclaiming 'Dear, oh dear!' Palace sources dismissed the idea that there was any criticism of the prime minister implied in his conversational openers. Meanwhile, the pound continued to hover at exchange rates (against the dollar) that were the lowest seen in more than 35 years. This, in turn, increased the government's cost of borrowing, and on 14 October the Bank of England's intervention to buy government bonds ended. Sterling seemed to be in a parlous state.

14 October 2022
Nicola Jennings
Guardian

On 2 October, Liz Truss had told the BBC's Laura Kuenssberg that axeing the 45-pence income tax rate was 'a decision that the chancellor made', even though the government's economic plans were widely seen as an expression of 'Trussonomics'. Asked on 13 October whether he would remain as chancellor, Kwarteng told the BBC: '100 per cent: I'm not going anywhere.' On 14 October, Truss sacked him, as she abandoned yet more of the mini budget. 'I have', she announced, 'acted decisively today, because my priority is ensuring our country's economic stability.' Her own stability and authority, though, seemed more precarious than ever.

15 October 2022
Brian Adcock
Guardian

The appointment of Jeremy Hunt as the new chancellor was a signal to the Conservative Party, the country and the international markets that the Trussonomic revolution was dead in the water. By 17 October, Hunt had effectively shredded the Kwarteng mini budget and the platform that won Truss the leadership. He cancelled most of the proposed tax cuts (including a drop in the basic rate of income tax to 19 per cent), limited the subsidies of the Energy Price Guarantee (which the prime minister had repeatedly championed) to six months rather than two years and hinted a new windfall tax was on the table (a move that Truss had previously said she would not countenance).

18 October 2022
Ella Baron
Guardian

With her economic strategy in tatters, Liz Truss's authority was draining away. As the cartoonist saw it, 'In the aftermath of the Kwarteng budget disaster and the weakening of Liz Truss, new chancellor Jeremy Hunt is now seen as virtually unsackable, while Truss's future seems to hang in the balance. His primary purpose is to put out the fires started by the government and restore credibility to the UK economy. But in doing so, will he put out the embers of Truss's reign too?'

21 October 2022
Andy Davey
Jewish Chronicle

As Truss's fate hung in the balance, she suffered the further indignity of unflattering comparisons to a lettuce. As described by the *Daily Star*, 'Last Friday (October 14) we pitted a lettuce from Tesco against the wet lettuce PM, seeing whether it would decay before Truss lost her job.' The newspaper trained a webcam on the 60p vegetable, which acquired 'googly eyes' and a blond wig. On 20 October, as the *Star* described, viewers 'saw the lettuce be crowned victor, celebrating with a glass of prosecco and a Greggs sausage roll'. And the national anthem played. That day, Liz Truss announced she would resign.

21 October 2022
Dave Brown
Independent

23 October 2022
Steve Bright
Sun

Following Liz Truss's resignation, Boris Johnson flew back from his holiday in the Caribbean in order to make a bid to return to Downing Street, despite only resigning as prime minister in early July. Johnson's allies said that he 'easily' had enough support to be a strong contender and was the only candidate who could win a general election against the Labour Party. But critics argued that re-electing Johnson would only cause further scandal given the pending Partygate investigations. Former party leader William Hague said that bringing Johnson back would cause a 'death spiral' for the Conservative Party.

Liz Truss's previous rival for the Conservative leadership, Rishi Sunak, appeared to lead the field to succeed her as prime minister. There was also support for Penny Mordaunt, leader of the House of Commons, while some MPs wanted a Boris Johnson comeback. To try and avoid another lengthy leadership election – the last one had taken three months – the party's 1922 Committee had put in place a truncated timescale and the stipulation that any candidate would need at least 100 nominations to stand. With Labour enjoying 30-plus percentage-point leads in the polls, some even wondered whether the Conservative Party was heading for extinction.

24 October 2022
Nicola Jennings
Guardian

Liz Truss made history when she visited Buckingham Palace, on 25 October, for her final audience with King Charles, to submit her formal resignation. Having occupied Number 10 for 45 days, she was the shortest-serving British prime minister ever. (The runner-up is George Canning, at 119 days, but he was not deposed: in 1827, he died in office.) In the end, there was no overt Boris Johnson comeback bid, amid reports of his support being soft. Penny Mordaunt fell short of the 100-nomination threshold, delivering victory to Rishi Sunak – the fifth prime minister in eight years, but the first ever prime minister of South Asian and Hindu heritage.

25 October 2022
Steven Camley
Herald Scotland

Rishi Sunak promised a government of integrity but reappointed Suella Braverman as home secretary, just days after Liz Truss had accepted her resignation over a security breach involving emails. Braverman was criticised in Parliament over failures to control 'irregular' migration in small boats, and over the desperate overcrowding at the Manston migrant centre in Kent, which had been firebombed. Challenging her critics to 'get rid of me', she described the migrants and refugees as an 'invasion', causing uproar. Sunak insisted, at cabinet, that the UK was a 'compassionate, welcoming country'.

2 November 2022
Dave Brown
Independent

The UK had hosted the 2021 international climate-change conference COP26, at which the then Prince Charles – a long-time environmentalist – and Boris Johnson had addressed attendees. Eyebrows were raised at reports that the government had informed King Charles he should not attend the 2022 COP27, and that even Rishi Sunak would be absent. But, according to the cartoonist, 'after some threats by Boris Johnson that he would attend . . . and a public ban on King Charles attending, and then some drawn-out will-he-won't-he dithering, Rishi Sunak decided he needed to be seen at COP27 after all.'

5 November 2022
Andy Davey
Daily Telegraph

The media made much of Rishi Sunak's supposed 'snub' of ex-minister Matt Hancock, when he had not shaken hands with him as MPs greeted his arrival at Number 10. A week later, the Conservative Party removed the whip from Hancock. His offence was to join contestants on the reality show *I'm a Celebrity . . . Get Me Out of Here!*. As the BBC put it, 'Mr Hancock will swap representing his constituents at Westminster for eating bugs in the jungle in Australia.' Hancock earned widespread criticism for his decision, while the prime minister's spokesman insisted that 'at a challenging time for the country, MPs should be working hard for their constituents.'

6 November 2022
Steven Camley
Herald Scotland

By November, the number of 'irregular arrivals' into the UK – migrants, asylum seekers and refugees on small boats – was reaching 40,000 for 2022. That was 10,000 more than the total for 2021, and 30,000 more than the number of those taking to sea in 2018. Just three nationalities made up half the numbers over those five years: Afghans, Iranians – and more recently, Albanians. The statistics alone suggested that government polices to deter people-smuggling were failing. The cartoon features unsuccessful cross-Channel invaders from history, including King Philip II of Spain, whose Spanish Armada so spectacularly failed in 1588.

7 November 2022
Steve Bright
Sun

Rishi Sunak's colleagues seemed to ensnare him in another controversy, when it emerged that Cabinet Office minister Gavin Williamson had sent abusive text messages in September to the former chief whip Wendy Morton, venting frustration that he had not been invited to the Queen's funeral. His closing remarks were: 'Well let's see how many more times you fuck us all over. There is a price for everything.' The price for Williamson was resignation, on 8 November. He had previously been sacked from government by Boris Johnson, and earlier by Theresa May – around which time, his pet tarantula had made headlines.

8 November 2022
Christian Adams
Evening Standard

13 November 2022
Morten Morland
The Times

A convincing re-election victory on 9 November for Ron DeSantis as governor of Florida strengthened his position should he, as was widely suggested, try to become the Republican Party's presidential candidate in 2024. A seemingly rattled Donald Trump – expected to announce his own bid to be the party's presidential candidate – told journalists on his plane that if DeSantis ran, 'he could hurt himself very badly. I think the base would not like it.' He also hinted that he had information on the governor that 'won't be very flattering'.

Ahead of the chancellor's Autumn Statement on 17 November, widely trailed reports suggested that Jeremy Hunt would offer up a bumper crop of spending cuts and tax increases to address the so-called 'black hole' in government finances estimated at £55–£60 billion. According to the *Daily Mirror*, the accounting firm RSM was warning against 'austerity mark 2', in reference to the era of austerity that had unfolded under Chancellor George Osborne a decade earlier, in the wake of the 2008–10 financial crash.

14 November 2022
Rob Murray
Daily Telegraph

Politics entered sport when the 2022 FIFA World Cup opened in Qatar. According to the cartoonist, 'The Iran football team were incredibly brave to not sing their national anthem at the World Cup match against England, as a sign of solidarity with the protestors back home. When they did sing at the next game, it's easy to think "Pathetic – if you're going to mount a protest, stick with it". But these people have all got families at home and the screws would have been turned on them. It wouldn't surprise me at all if they were told "Unless you sing, it won't end well."'

23 November 2022
Peter Brookes
The Times

Rishi Sunak's government had insisted that a bill drafted by Nicola Sturgeon's Scottish Nationalist government, to hold another referendum on Scottish independence in 2023, was illegitimate. The reason given was that the union of Scotland and England was not a 'devolved matter', but rather of UK-wide significance, and so any decision to hold a referendum was 'reserved' for Westminster politicians. The Scottish government appealed to the UK Supreme Court, on the basis that a referendum was advisory only; but on 23 November, the appeal was unanimously rejected. It seemed that on this issue Sturgeon was, for now, silenced.

24 November 2022
Dave Brown
Independent

25 November 2022
Andy Davey
Daily Telegraph

Jeremy Hunt's Autumn Statement promised to extend the subsidies of Liz Truss's Energy Price Guarantee for another year, beyond April 2023, despite expected rises in energy prices. The chancellor urged citizens to 'take responsibility' for energy use as part of a 'national mission'. As the cartoonist put it, the chancellor 'said people should cut their energy use to stop the UK being "blackmailed" by Vladimir Putin. There was a public information campaign to encourage people to turn down boilers, switch off radiators and take showers, not baths. How far will this go?'

The consumer organisation Which? issued an alarming report suggesting that 31 per cent of single parents had skipped meals because of the steeply rising cost of food, as did 14 per cent of all those included in its survey. Given the lower levels of disposable income available to poorer households, they were seeing a disproportionate amount of their resources swallowed up by food and energy costs. Which? quoted one father, Paul, saying: 'I sometimes go without eating as I prioritise for my son. I've lost a lot of weight since April.'

25 November 2022
Ben Jennings
Guardian

27 November 2022
Chris Riddell
Observer

Rishi Sunak's commitment to a government of integrity, professionalism and accountability was sorely tested by skeletons coming out of the closet. He appointed a lawyer to investigate bullying complaints against Deputy Prime Minister and Justice Secretary Dominic Raab. Levelling-Up Secretary Michael Gove was being scrutinised in connection with the fast-tracking of contracts for personal protective equipment (PPE) to a company recommended by Tory peer Lady Michelle Mone – known as Baroness Bra, for her lingerie brand. And the criticism of Suella Braverman rumbled on, after she declared that it was her 'dream' and 'obsession' to send asylum seekers to Rwanda.

Writing in the *Daily Telegraph* that the installation of Rishi Sunak and Jeremy Hunt at the top of government represented a 'coup', arch-Brexiteer Nigel Farage went on to add: 'The conditions for a new insurgency in British politics are ripe.' Farage, now 'honorary president' of the Reform UK Party he founded, claimed that 'thousands of Conservatives' had joined in recent weeks. He alleged that 'British citizens' felt 'confusion and anger' at seeing 'young men from different cultures hanging around' – and promised that Reform UK would field 'a full slate' of candidates at the next general election.

28 November 2022
Steve Bright
Sun

30 November 2022
Patrick Blower
Daily Telegraph

Modern Britain was giving up on Christianity as its majority religion in favour of secularism, according to results revealed from the 2021 Census. Those identifying as Christian had shrunk from 59.3 per cent in the 2011 Census to 46.2 per cent. By contrast, those identifying as having no religious affiliation had shot up by 8.5 million people, to 37.5 per cent of the population. The decline of Christian values caused the *Telegraph*'s Madeline Grant to speculate that Britain was being reduced to 'snarky faux-communities of social media, or cult-like devotions to contemporary fads'.

Harry and Meghan, the Duke and Duchess of Sussex, had signed a five-year deal for $100 million with streaming company Netflix, including for a six-part autobiographical documentary series. A surprise trailer was released on 1 December – coinciding with a US visit by William and Kate, the Prince and Princess of Wales – in which, amid a montage of personal photographs, the duchess could be seen wiping away tears, while at one point the duke said: 'No one sees what is happening behind closed doors.' It ended with the duchess tantalising the viewer: 'When the stakes are this high, doesn't it make sense to hear our story from us?'

2 December 2022
Christian Adams
Evening Standard

When the results of some internal Russian government polling were leaked abroad, they showed that only 27 per cent of Russians backed the fight against Ukraine. As the cartoonist put it, 'Support for the war in Ukraine had fallen dramatically according to a leaked poll. The wives and mothers of young Russian soldiers had begun to realise that their offspring were returning from the "special military operation" in body bags. The babushkas' revolt put further pressure on Putin. I've always loved the sweeping graphic power of Soviet propaganda art, so any excuse to borrow it is welcome.'

2 December 2022
Andy Davey
Daily Telegraph

THEY'RE CHANGING THE OLD GUARD AT BUCKINGHAM PALACE...

When the British-born, black charity founder Ngozi Fulani attended a palace reception, she was grilled by the 83-year-old Lady Susan Hussey on her origins: 'Where do you *really* come from?' Forced to issue an apology, Lady Susan temporarily stood down as an honorary lady of the household. The cartoonist thought Fulani's treatment amounted to 'pure and absolute condescension'. He added: 'I got hundreds of complaints from *Times* readers . . . "How dare you treat an old woman like that?" . . . I'd say, in this age of equality, I can have a go at her as much as I can at an 80-year-old man [meaning Joe Biden]; and why aren't you defending the person she behaved unspeakably to?'

2 December 2022
Peter Brookes
The Times

3 December 2022
Kevin Kallaugher
Economist

Although China had developed its own vaccine against Covid-19, it had relied largely on a zero-tolerance policy, employing mass testing and local lockdowns to try and nip any outbreak in the bud. The strict policy, however, had brought severe social and economic disruption and stress, and when some quarantined Chinese died in a fire, a rising tide of protest began to acquire a more general anti-government flavour. As a result, Chinese premier Xi Jinping relented, and an end to the mass testing and lockdown strategy was promised. But that also potentially threatened new outbreaks in an under-vaccinated population.

Former prime minister Gordon Brown had prepared a report for the Labour Party entitled *A New Britain*, published in December. It promised a raft of reforms to devolve power away from Westminster to the cities, regions and nations of the United Kingdom. It also advocated doing away with the unelected House of Lords and replacing it with an elected chamber. An enthusiastic Sir Keir Starmer publicly endorsed the report, promising that its changes could be implemented within one five-year parliament. However, history was also littered with failed and abandoned proposals to reform the House of Lords.

6 December 2022
Morten Morland
The Times

BARONESS MONE LEAVES LORDS to CLEAR HER NAME
HELLE
9020
2413

7 December 2022
Steven Camley
Herald Scotland

When the House of Lords commissioners for standards announced an investigation into the business activities of Lady Mone, the Conservative peer took a 'leave of absence'. Allegedly, she had failed to declare her own financial interest in the firm Medpro, which she had recommended be fast-tracked to provide personal protective equipment in 2020. The company had won a contract worth £200 million, and reporting from the *Guardian* claimed that Mone had earned £29 million. The cartoonist imagines that she – no stranger to reality TV – might be escaping the political jungle for the *I'm a Celebrity* jungle.

Planned strikes proliferated across industries and professions, from rail staff to nurses, postal workers to driving instructors, as some commentators began describing December as a new 'Winter of Discontent'. The Met Office's chief meteorologist informed the public that 'an Arctic maritime airmass' meant that 'UK temperatures will fall with widespread overnight frosts, severe in places, and daytime temperatures only a few degrees above freezing.' A yellow weather warning was issued, as well as a 'Level Three Cold Weather Alert'.

12 December 2022
Christian Adams
Evening Standard

When the RMT rail union went on strike on 13 December, it was the first of 12 planned strike days over December. On BBC Radio 4's *Today* (6 December), RMT leader Mick Lynch defended the strikes and complained of 'a generalised attack on working people' who were seeing 'their wages lowered against inflation and often their conditions ripped up'. In the cartoonist's view, 'All the working practices the RMT's Mick Lynch wants to endure are antiquated, so I drew him on Stephenson's *Rocket. The Times* got a letter about a "serious mistake" in this: "Mick Lynch would not have been standing alone on the footplate." Quite right!'

14 December 2022
Peter Brookes
The Times

Sixty-nine Conservative MPs backed an unsuccessful private members' bill that would have forced the government to ignore rulings of the European Court of Human Rights, when it came to the policy of sending asylum seekers to Rwanda. Suella Braverman, as a cabinet minister, could not vote for it – but it was well known that she wanted to withdraw the UK from the European Convention on Human Rights. Meanwhile, as Rishi Sunak accused Sir Keir Starmer of being too 'weak' to stand up to striking unions, the official Labour stance still pulled back from endorsing any particular strike actions.

15 December 2022
Steve Bell
Guardian

In the first week of December, the ambulance service, from paramedics to call handlers, agreed to go on strike later in the month – though they would still handle life-threatening emergencies. According to the cartoonist, 'NHS bosses urged hospitals to free up beds to prepare for "extensive disruption" caused by ambulance staff strikes. Rishi Sunak's spokesman said the number of ambulances available to attend calls would be reduced "significantly". Armed forces were made ready for deployment to hospital trusts ahead of the strikes.'

18 December 2022
Andy Davey
Daily Telegraph

As talks collapsed between the health secretary, Steven Barclay, and the union Unite, representing National Health Service workers, Rishi Sunak defended the government's refusal to
enter pay negotiations or accede to pay demands, instead stressing the role of the independent NHS Pay Review Body. Meanwhile, he had already endorsed plans for a large-scale
coronation for King Charles III, describing it as 'a unique moment for the country'. The
Guardian estimated that the coronation of Queen Elizabeth II, in 1953, cost the equivalent
of £27 million – a figure that would surely be dwarfed by the pomp and pageantry in 2023.

21 December 2022
Steve Bell
Guardian

22 December 2022
Dave Brown
Independent

On the day before the ambulance service strike, Health Minister Will Quince advised the public to take 'extra care' on 21 December, having already said that people should avoid 'risky activities' and unnecessary driving. Meanwhile, the NHS medical director, Professor Stephen Powis, was urging people to 'drink responsibly' and avoid dialling 999 unless the situation was life-threatening. But still, Rishi Sunak appeared to be on a collision course with NHS workers over pay.

In King Charles's first Christmas Day address, he lauded 'the extraordinary ability of each person to touch, with goodness and compassion, the lives of others', paying tribute to 'all those wonderfully kind people who so generously give food or donations ... to support those around them in greatest need'. Meanwhile, in the run up to Christmas, Rishi Sunak seemed bizarrely out of touch when asking a homeless man at a shelter: 'Do you work in business?' Labour described the encounter as 'excruciating'.

26 December 2022
Rebecca Hendin
Guardian

House of Commons research suggested that the chancellor's decision in the Autumn Statement to freeze income tax thresholds until 2028 would deprive a dual-income household earning £60,000 of more than £40,000 over a decade – compared to what they *would* have earned, had thresholds risen in line with inflation. The *Daily Telegraph* called the measures 'stealth taxes' on the middle class. The well-known satirical sketch 'Class' was broadcast on *The Frost Report* in 1966. Its line-up featured a tall John Cleese (upper class), the middling-height Ronnie Barker (middle class) and the short Ronnie Corbett (working class).

28 December 2022
Rob Murray
Daly Telegraph

Despite the Conservative Party traditionally being the 'party of law and order', reducing crime has been an elusive goal for politicians of all stripes. Labour now proposed to revive Tony Blair's 'tough on crime, tough on the causes of crime' slogan and prioritise crime prevention. One element involved creating 'community payback boards' to oversee a wider range of community sentences. According to the cartoonist, 'When it comes to law and order stories, the scales and sword of justice are often first to come to mind. A bit of a tired old cliché. Combining it with the legend of King Arthur and Excalibur gives it a fresh twist.'

30 December 2022
Peter Schrank
The Times

In his first speech of 2023, Rishi Sunak emphasised his ambition for all young people to 'study some form of maths' up to the age of 18, adding: 'This is personal for me. Every opportunity I've had in life began with the education I was so fortunate to receive.' According to the government, 8 million British adults 'had the numeracy skills of primary school children'. Meanwhile, one hospital chief spoke to ITV News of the pressure on accident and emergency departments as a 'matter of life and death', with some patients waiting hours in ambulances or in corridors.

5 January 2023
Ben Jennings
Guardian

In his own first speech of 2023, Sir Keir Starmer cheekily stole the 2016 Brexit Leave campaign's slogan when he promised – assuming he won the next general election – to introduce a 'take back control' bill. Its aim, he said, would be to devolve a wide range of powers away from Westminster to local and regional government, and, in the process, implicitly dilute Labour's association with 'socialist' central planning. But, by avoiding discussion of the effects of Brexit (Labour) or the legacy of 12 years in charge (Conservative), both party leaders seemed to have large elephants in the room.

8 January 2023
Chris Riddell
Observer

'Let us come together and show this country in 2023 that it is Conservatives who deliver at every level of government.' That was Rishi Sunak's message, stressing 'family' to followers of the Conservative Home website. Yet, a new grouping called the Conservative Democratic Organisation aimed to empower the Boris Johnson-loving grassroots members, amid rumours of a possible Johnson resurgence. The disaffected ex-minister Nadine Dorries – an ardent admirer of Johnson – told her party: 'It's bring back Boris or die.' Meanwhile, Prince Harry's forthcoming autobiography *Spare* promised to lay bare dysfunctional family relationships.

9 January 2023
Patrick Blower
Daily Telegraph

On 8 January, supporters of Brazil's defeated ex-president Jair Bolsonaro tried to storm the country's Congress building, along with the presidential palace and the Brazilian Supreme Court. They wanted to overturn the narrow electoral victory of Luiz Inácio Lula da Silva, on a day of unrest that was immediately compared with the American insurrection of 6 January 2021, following Donald Trump's own failure to get re-elected. The most colourful US insurrectionist on 6 January, with his furry horned headdress, had been Jacob Chansley, who then served gaol time.

10 January 2023
Morten Morland
The Times

The Church of England Commissioners published a 'full report' into the Church's historic involvement in the slave trade, in the shape of 'Queen Anne's Bounty' – a fund established in 1704, intended to subsidise poorer clergy. It was later rolled into the modern Church Commissioners' endowment funds. Justin Welby, the archbishop of Canterbury, described the discovery of the true nature of the 'predecessor fund' as shaming, writing: 'I am deeply sorry for these links.' The Church promised a sum of £100 million to address past wrongs by way of 'investment, research and engagement'.

12 January 2023
Patrick Blower
Daily Telegraph

During Prime Minister's Questions in the House of Commons, the famously wealthy Rishi Sunak asserted that he was, in fact, registered with an NHS doctor, though he acknowledged he had used 'independent healthcare' in the past. He had recently been unforthcoming about whether he had an NHS GP. The cartoon has Sunak surrounded by an army of MPs in the image of Business and Energy Secretary Grant Shapps. In reality, Shapps missed the session, following the embarrassing revelation that he had airbrushed Boris Johnson out of a 2022 publicity photo he posted to his Twitter account.

12 January 2023
Steve Bell
Guardian

14 January 2023
Andy Davey
Daily Telegraph

New figures out from the Office of National Statistics described UK GDP in the fourth quarter of 2022 as 'flat'. The only straw to be clutched by the prime minister or his chancellor seemed to be one temporary improvement. In the cartoonist's words, 'The UK economy unexpectedly grew 0.1 per cent in November 2022, helped by a boost from the football World Cup. Pubs and restaurants contributed to growth as people went out to watch games and get slaughtered to forget the miserable government.' December 2022 brought a 0.5 per cent slump in GDP, as the Christmas boom failed to materialise.

On 16 January, confidence in London's Metropolitan Police was dealt a serious blow when the suspended PC David Carrick pleaded guilty to 49 charges of rape and sexual assault, as well as false imprisonment and coercive control. He was arrested in October 2021, but had committed the offences over 17 years while a serving officer. No action had been taken over earlier allegations against him, because his victims feared his threats and were too afraid to give evidence. The Met's recently appointed commissioner, Sir Mark Rowley, promised: 'I'm going to put in place ruthless systems to squeeze out those who shouldn't be with us.'

19 January 2023
Ben Jennings
Guardian

20 January 2023
Christian Adams
Evening Standard

As the war in Ukraine ground on, representatives of around 50 countries met at the US Air Base at Ramstein, Germany. Led by the United States and other NATO countries, they agreed a multi-billion-dollar package of military assistance for the government in Kyiv, including heavy weapons and air defences. The UK would be providing Challenger 2 tanks. But there was criticism of Germany's flaccid equivocations when Defence Minister Boris Pistorius said: 'We still cannot say when a decision will be taken, or what the decision will be' about allowing Ukraine the use of German-made Leopard tanks.

RUNNING ON EMPTY...

On 19 January, the charismatic New Zealand prime minister, Jacinda Ardern, surprised her country and the world by announcing her resignation. She had led her Labour government for nearly six years, including through crises of domestic terrorism and Covid-19. In an emotional speech, she said: 'I know that I no longer have enough in the tank,' adding: 'I am human, politicians are human. We give all that we can for as long as we can. And then it's time.' Meanwhile, some felt that the UK's Conservative government, haunted by the shadow of Boris Johnson, had run out of life and ideas.

20 January 2023
Dave Brown
Independent

The government released a video featuring Rishi Sunak, in the back of a chauffeur-driven car, enthusing about the second tranche of the Levelling Up Fund for 'investing in local areas'. However, the message was overshadowed by observations that the prime minister was not wearing a seatbelt while talking to camera, and thus breaking the law. A chastened Sunak admitted his 'error of judgement', as Lancashire Police imposed a fixed penalty notice, his second in government. This was, though, vastly cheaper than the seven-figure penalty that Conservative chairman Nadhim Zahawi had reportedly had to pay to settle his tax affairs.

24 January 2023
Steven Camley
Herald Scotland

Michael Gove made a speech to various local leaders assembling for the 'Convention of the North', welcoming £2.1 billion from the Levelling Up Fund. But there were accusations of favouritism in the allocations and complaints that areas of evident deprivation were left out, such as Rochdale, Middlesbrough or parts of Tyneside. According to *The Times*, twice as many Conservative as Labour constituencies received money. In the 1968 film *Oliver!*, based on Dickens's *Oliver Twist*, the hungry boy-hero walks up to the workhouse beadle, Mr Bumble, meekly asking for 'more' gruel, only to be shouted at.

27 January 2023
Graeme Bandeira
Northern Agenda

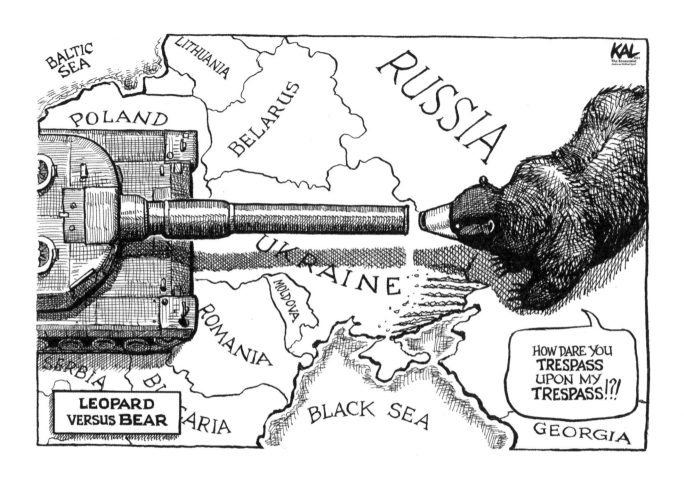

27 January 2023
Kevin Kallaugher
Economist

On 24 January, the German chancellor, Olaf Scholz, finally put his seal of approval on sending some German-made Leopard 2 tanks to the Ukrainian army. The decision also freed up allies such as Poland, Norway, Spain and the Netherlands to transfer some of their own Leopards to Ukraine, since they needed German permission to export them. In what seemed a coordinated change of policy, the United States agreed that it would send some of its Abrams tanks for Ukrainian use, having originally demurred.

Although Jeremy Hunt's Autumn Statement of 2022 had confirmed that work was to continue on HS2 – the high-speed rail line connecting London and Manchester – new doubts arose about whether it would reach its planned southern terminus at Euston station or must be permanently curtailed in London's suburbs. High inflation was ramping up costs on the huge project. On 27 January, Hunt sought to quash doubts by insisting that he could imagine no 'conceivable circumstance' preventing the line reaching Euston.

27 January 2023
David Simonds
Evening Standard

The chancellor spoke to *The Times* about the many thousands of over-50s who had left the workforce since Covid-19 struck. According to the cartoonist, 'Jeremy Hunt got a bit panicky because we seemed to have lost a million or so of the workforce. Nothing to do with Brexit, obviously. It must be those over-50 work-shy slackers who decided to take retirement rather than work for ever-less money. He urged them to get off the golf course because his long-term vision – ah, that's why his eyes follow you around! – is focused on growth . . . or something.'

29 January 2023
Andy Davey
Daily Telegraph

On 29 January, Rishi Sunak sacked Nadhim Zahawi as Conservative chairman for 'a serious breach of the Ministerial Code', following an investigation by his independent ethics advisor, Laurie Magnus. The issue at stake for Zahawi – who had served briefly as chancellor under Boris Johnson – was his complex tax affairs. Having used lawyers to characterise questions over his taxable liabilities as 'smears', Zahawi was judged to have made misleading statements. It was confirmed that His Majesty's Revenue and Customs had issued him a late-payment fine of more than £1 million and demanded the overdue capital gains tax. Zahawi claimed his error was 'careless and not deliberate'.

30 January 2023
Nicola Jennings
Guardian

3 February 2023
Ben Jennings
Guardian

The energy and fuel giant Shell plc announced the highest profits in its 115-year history. They had more than doubled on the previous year's, to £32.2 billion, after Russia's invasion of Ukraine had sent global oil and gas prices soaring. 'We intend to remain disciplined,' the company said, 'while delivering compelling shareholder returns.' Opposition politicians pushed for extending windfall taxes on oil and gas companies, as the war continued to extract its toll in human lives.

The publication of company accounts for the Turnberry golf course (and other Scottish assets) owned by Donald Trump and his family showed a loss in 2022 of £15 million. Meanwhile British Gas and other energy companies had been excoriated for the practice of forcibly entering the homes of some of their most vulnerable customers in order to install pre-payment meters for those in arrears. On 2 February, the energy regulator Ofgem banned the practice, while the government put pressure on British Gas's owners, Centrica, to outline how they would compensate customers.

3 February 2023
Steven Camley
Herald Scotland

GETTING BACK ON THE HORSE...

5 · 2 · 23

Despite the fact that her brief prime ministership had fallen off the cliff edge, Liz Truss had – according to sources quoted by *The Times* – 'half a hope' of returning as Conservative leader in opposition, should the circumstances present themselves. While understanding that she had 'lost the battle', she also regarded politics as 'a long game'. For Sean O'Grady, writing in the *Independent*, the idea of a Truss comeback was 'an absurd proposition'. 'If they want a disaster back,' he wrote, 'then they can get Boris Johnson, who does it much better.'

5 February 2023
Morten Morland
The Times

On 2 February, members of the Royal College of Nursing (RCN) delivered a petition to Number 10 signed by 100,000 NHS staff, patients and members of the public, demanding that the government's number-crunching produce an acceptable wage settlement. Ahead of further strikes, involving both nurses and paramedics, the RCN claimed that since Sunak became prime minister, 'over 10,000 more patients per month are regularly waiting over 12 hours for treatment in A&E'. According to Patricia Marquis, the RCN's director for England, 'Patients are not dying because nurses are striking. Nurses are striking because patients are dying.'

5 February 2023
Nicola Jennings
Guardian

9 February 2023
Steve Bell
Guardian

While prime minister, and afterwards, Boris Johnson had been one of the most vocal supporters of Ukraine among international leaders. During a surprise visit to London on 8 February, President Zelensky addressed assembled parliamentarians in Westminster Hall and publicly thanked Johnson: 'You got others united when it seemed absolutely impossible.' Sunak promised Zelensky more training for military pilots and marines, but fell short of offering the warplanes that the president wanted.

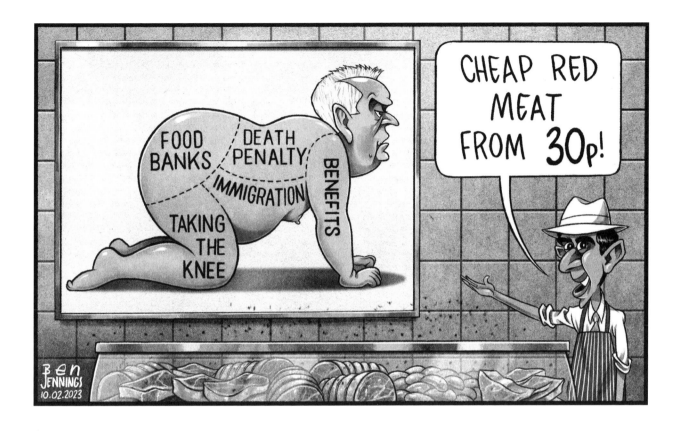

The appointment of Lee Anderson MP as the new Conservative deputy chairman was interpreted as an attempt to connect with 2019 Conservative voters from so-called 'Red Wall' constituencies in the English North and Midlands. This ex-miner, an unashamed culture warrior, had claimed that foodbanks were over-used (because meals could be cooked for '30p') and recently backed the death penalty. Of this cartoon, he tweeted: 'Typical of how the left will exaggerate to personally attack people. This deepy [*sic*] offensive & hurtful cartoon shows me with an extended earlobe. This is not the case at all & the artist should apologise. The rest is ok.'

10 February 2023
Ben Jennings
Guardian

Nicola Sturgeon, first minister of Scotland, unexpectedly announced her decision to quit politics, which, she acknowledged, 'takes its toll on you and those around you'. Her nine years as leader of the Scottish National Party (SNP) had still not delivered her dream of an independent Scotland. On the same day, 15 February, the film star Raquel Welch died, aged 82. She had donned a memorable and minimal deerskin bikini for the prehistory-based British film *One Million Years B.C.* (1968). Here, Sturgeon replaces Welch, in homage to that film's poster.

16 February 2023
Christian Adams
Evening Standard

84

British Gas owners Centrica grabbed headlines when the company posted profits for 2022 of more than £3 billion, effectively tripling its 2021 profits. It threw into stark relief the company's recently banned practice of employing debt collectors to force struggling consumers onto pre-payment meters. And, as with Shell, the scale of the profits prompted calls for much more profound windfall taxes on energy companies. British Gas's advertising campaign in the 1990s had featured the catchphrase 'Don't you just love being in control?', as celebrities – such as Joan Collins – gave the thumbs-up and a flame miraculously flickered from their raised thumb.

17 February 2023
Dave Brown
Independent

STATE OF THE NATION...

ADAMS 23
21-02

Vladimir Putin used his annual address to the Russian Parliament to frame his perspective on current events. He railed against the West and the Ukrainian government, blaming both of them for the war – while excusing the people of Ukraine, who were 'hostages of the Kiev regime'. Western values of democracy and freedom were, he said, just a smokescreen for totalitarian values, and for Russia the war was a fight for survival. He also found time to attack the Anglican Church and to insist that, in the West, child abuse 'as far as paedophilia' was 'declared normal'.

21 February 2023
Christian Adams
Evening Standard

In 2019, Home Secretary Sajid Javid had stripped Shamima Begum of her British citizenship, after she and two friends had made their way to war-torn Syria, aged just 15, to join ISIS (Islamic State). Since 2019, she had languished in a detention camp in north-east Syria. On 22 February, lawyers working on her appeal failed to get her citizenship restored. The judge found 'credible suspicion' that she had been trafficked for 'sexual exploitation' – but argued that any decision to overturn the home secretary's decision, made on national security grounds, must rest with the Home Office.

23 February 2023
Dave Brown
Independent

25 February 2023
Dave Brown
Independent

UK supermarkets placed limits on the sale of some fruits and vegetables after bad weather in Spain and north Africa led to shortages. Environment Secretary Therese Coffey insisted that the food system remained 'resilient'. Responding to the predicament in the Commons, Coffey said that we should 'cherish' seasonal foods and, if we did, 'a lot of people would be eating turnips right now, rather than thinking necessarily about aspects of lettuce.' The Liberal Democrat leader, Ed Davey, regarded this as a 'let them eat turnips' attitude, in reference to the phrase 'Let them eat cake' supposedly uttered during a bread shortage by the Queen of France, Marie Antoinette.

The British government announced a national one-minute silence to 'pay tribute to the bravery of Ukrainians', marking 'a year since Russia's barbaric full-scale invasion'. In Ukraine itself, people remembered those lost, and everywhere the nation's blue and yellow flags flew, while buildings were illuminated in the national colours. An official Ukrainian video, *The Year of Invincibility*, marked 12 months of defiance, against the odds, and on social media President Zelensky promised victory. Putin's 'special military operation', intended as a swift instrument of regime change, had instead brought a bloody war of attrition and made him an international pariah.

26 February 2023
Chris Riddell
Observer

Belltoons.co.uk ©Steve Bell 2023 - 28-2 - 4735 -

28 February 2023
Steve Bell
Guardian

King Charles met with the president of the European Commission, Ursula von der Leyen, after the announcement of the EU–UK 'Windsor Framework' – mechanisms intended to reform the Northern Ireland Protocol agreed under Boris Johnson, and so resolve the province's post-Brexit difficulties. The meeting prompted a furious response from Sammy Wilson, Brexit spokesman for the Democratic Unionist Party. He told the *Daily Telegraph*'s 'Chopper' podcast that Charles was 'politicising the monarchy' and would 'come to regret' the meeting, since the DUP was still in dispute with the UK government and opposed to both the Northern Ireland Protocol and the Windsor Framework.

The Moral High Ground... ..alias a Toadstool upon a Dunghill.

When former health secretary Matt Hancock collaborated with journalist Isabel Oakeshott on his book *Pandemic Diaries* (2022), he handed her his WhatsApp messages. But Oakeshott then gave them to the *Daily Telegraph*, prompting Hancock to accuse her of a 'massive betrayal and breach of trust'. Messages revealed arguments over pandemic testing, Hancock's view of teaching unions as 'arses' and his mocking of Rishi Sunak's 'Eat Out to Help Out' scheme. The cartoonist alludes to James Gillray's cartoon (1791) entitled 'An excrescence; a fungus; alias a toad-stool upon a dung-hill', which satirised both Prime Minister William Pitt (the Younger) and King George III.

3 March 2023
Dave Brown
Independent

6 March 2023
Joe Lawrence
Guardian

The new Illegal Migration Bill proposed to deter 'unlawful migration' and require the 'removal' of illegal arrivals 'to their home country or to a safe third country to have their asylum claim processed'. In the cartoonist's words, 'Sunak is King Cnut in a futile attempt at holding back the waves (originally I was going to have "Our Mighty Cnut" as a title). He started to use stronger anti-immigration language, I assume to keep the far right of the party happy . . . he has a racist dog whistle and red meat for the rabid Home Office attack dog, and amongst all of this is a happy little Farage dung beetle, revelling in all the muck.'

According to *The Times*, Boris Johnson was putting his own father, Stanley Johnson, forward for a knighthood, as part of a very sizeable resignation honours list from his time as prime minister. While the comparable lists put forward by his predecessors David Cameron and Theresa May contained 60 and 62 nominations respectively, Johnson's was thought to be much bigger – around 100 names. Johnson's brother, the ex-minister Jo Johnson, had already been ennobled as Lord Johnson of Marylebone. Of Stanley Johnson, Sir Keir Starmer commented: 'For services for what?'

7 March 2023
Morten Morland
The Times

7 March 2023
Kevin Kallaugher
Economist

Rupert Murdoch, the owner of Fox News, admitted during a sworn deposition that some of the network's most prominent stars had 'endorsed' the 'false notion of a stolen election' following the 2020 US presidential election. His remarks were revealed as part of a defamation lawsuit brought by Dominion Voting Systems against Fox News, which alleged that the network had helped spread the lie, propagated by Donald Trump, that Dominion's technology had miscounted votes in Joe Biden's favour. Internal Fox News documents suggested that senior staff were privately dismissive of Trump's claims about election fraud (Murdoch called them 'really crazy stuff') but nevertheless indulged them on air.

British and French leaders seemed to be singing from the same hymn sheet, as Rishi Sunak hailed the first bilateral summit in five years as 'a new beginning, an *entente* renewed'. Following discussions with President Emmanuel Macron, the UK agreed to pay France 500 million euros over three years for a range of measures intended to prevent small boats bringing 'irregular migrants' across the English Channel. There was also agreement on deepening the military links between the two countries. The day before, the UK's Eurovision organisers announced that the UK entrant (Mae Muller) had been selected for this year's competition.

9 March 2023
Christian Adams
Evening Standard

10 March 2023
Andy Davey
Jewish Chronicle

On 3 March, the House of Commons Privileges Committee set out the 'next steps' in its investigation of whether Boris Johnson's explanations about breaches of Covid-19 lockdown restrictions were misleading and constituted 'a contempt' of the House of Commons. The report found that 'the evidence strongly suggests that breaches of guidance would have been obvious to Mr Johnson at the time.' As the cartoonist put it, 'There were lots of stories of drink, shenanigans of a sexual nature and whatnot at the Downing Street parties, but Boris Johnson apparently did not see this.'

The BBC appeared to score an own goal after suspending *Match of the Day* presenter Gary Lineker for commenting on politics. He had tweeted that the government's Illegal Migration Bill was 'an immeasurably cruel policy . . . not dissimilar to that used by Germany in the 30s'. Fellow presenters and pundits boycotted flagship shows out of solidarity with Lineker, and BBC sports coverage saw a weekend of chaos. After the BBC director-general, Tim Davie, reinstated Lineker and agreed to an independent review of the corporation's social-media guidelines, his own position was called into question, amid accusations that Conservative politicians had leant on Davie to act against Lineker.

13 March 2023
Steve Bright
Sun

A week before the government's Spring Statement (the budget), friends of Prince Andrew told the *Daily Mail* he was 'bewildered' and feeling left 'in despair' that he had not so far received any share of the £650 million inheritance from his mother. According to the palace source, the Queen's wealth had passed from 'monarch to monarch' because that was the most 'tax efficient' way to transfer it. Legislation passed in 1993, under Prime Minister John Major, meant that inheritance tax did not have to be paid on transfer of assets from one sovereign to another. The Queen's other children had not, therefore, received a share of the inheritance.

14 March 2023
Steve Bell
Guardian

While some Conservatives were eager for the government to introduce tax cuts – and to abandon a scheduled rise in corporation tax to 25 per cent – there was little sign that Jeremy Hunt's impending budget would deliver what they wanted. Although Hunt had favoured lowering corporation tax during his brief foray into the Conservative leadership election in summer 2022, he insisted now that the priory was being 'responsible with public finances'. In January, he had hinted at cutting tax 'when the time is right' – interpreted as meaning spring 2024, in time for the next general election.

16 March 2023
Rob Murray
Daily Telegraph

RENDEZVOUS

With the US secretary of state already warning China against supplying weapons to Russia, Xi Jinping was about to arrive in Moscow on a state visit. The Chinese leader was, according to the cartoonist, 'likely to discuss sanctions evasion schemes' with Vladimir Putin and support the provision of Chinese equipment to Russia, via Belarus. The cartoon is a pastiche of David Low's famous 1939 cartoon 'Rendezvous' (published September 1939), in which the dictators Hitler and Stalin greet each other over a ruined landscape and the corpse of Poland, carved up between them.

19 March 2023
Andy Davey
Daily Telegraph

On 17 March, the International Criminal Court in The Hague issued an arrest warrant for Vladimir Putin, on charges of complicity in the illegal deportation of children from occupied Ukraine for 're-education' and adoption. Russia, which does not recognise the ICC, called the decision 'meaningless' – but it meant that Putin was theoretically liable to arrest should he go abroad. As if in defiance, on 19 March Putin made a surprise trip to Mariupol in eastern Ukraine, the city that, in 2022, became the symbol of the war's devastation and where – according to Ukrainian authorities – around 20,000 people had died.

20 March 2023
Ben Jennings
Guardian

In the cartoonist's words, 'The Parliamentary Privileges Committee retired in order to work out if Boris Johnson had recklessly misled, or intentionally misled, Parliament. A liar or a clown. Recklessness is more subjective, and so, perhaps, an easier conclusion. During the proceedings, Harriet Harman said: "If I was going 100mph and I saw the speedometer saying 100 miles an hour, it would be a bit odd, wouldn't it, if I said somebody assured me that I was not."' (In January 2003, Harman was banned from driving for seven days and fined £400 for speeding at 99mph on the M4: her solicitor said: 'She does not seek to make any excuse for the offence.')

24 March 2023
Andy Davey
Daily Telegraph

At the last minute, Emmanuel Macron postponed King Charles's state visit to France. This was due to the mass unrest caused by Macron's raising of the state retirement age from 62 to 64, without a parliamentary vote. According to the cartoonist, 'With the exception of the war in Ukraine, British cartoonists and editors are often not keen on covering the politics of continental Europe. I understand this: it's always more fun if there is a chance that your targets may actually see the cartoon. But as I grew up on the continent, I regret this. There was a British angle here, so I was glad to seize the opportunity.'

25 March 2023
Peter Schrank
The Times

The SNP elected Humza Yousaf to fill Nicola Sturgeon's shoes as party leader and Scotland's first minister. He was seen as the continuity candidate. His rivals had been Kate Forbes, Scotland's finance minister and a rising star, whose opposition to same-sex marriage had lost her supporters; and Ash Regan, who quit the government in opposition to proposed changes to gender recognition. The son of Asian immigrants, Yousaf celebrated with the words 'From the Punjab to our Parliament, this is a journey for our generations'. Polling showed support for Scottish independence slipping to 39 per cent from a record 58 per cent in 2020.

28 March 2023
Patrick Blower
Daily Telegraph

After the dissolution of the Soviet Union in 1991, monuments to Marxism-Leninism were pulled down across the ex-Soviet republics and unceremoniously dumped in temporary holding sites, like graveyards to the past. Now it seemed that Sir Keir Starmer was trying to consign his left-wing predecessor as Labour leader to history. On 28 March, the party's National Executive Committee passed Starmer's motion to block Jeremy Corbyn from standing as a Labour candidate at the next general election, on the basis that it would be 'detrimental' to Labour prospects. Corbyn, an MP since 1983, accused Starmer and the NEC of 'undermining the party's internal democracy'.

29 March 2023
Patrick Blower
Daily Telegraph

On 27 March, Benjamin Netanyahu, Israel's prime minister, bowed to massive public pressure and announced a pause in plans to rein in the power of the country's Supreme Court. He headed a fractious coalition government, reliant on small, extreme right-wing parties: they wanted the judicial changes because they saw the court as over-powerful and too 'left-wing'. But many Israelis saw the move as a threat to the country's democratic checks and balances. The result was weeks of protests and defections from government, as well as rumblings in the powerful military and a debilitating general strike.

29 March 2023
Peter Brookes
The Times

In January 2018, stories emerged of hush money paid – in 2016 – by Donald Trump to porn star 'Stormy Daniels' (Stephanie Clifford), to silence her about their sexual relationship a decade before. Trump denied everything, but on 30 March 2023 a grand jury in Manhattan voted for his indictment on charges of falsifying financial records relating to the alleged affair. Trump remained defiant but was arraigned in a New York courtroom four days later. In 2016, a recording went public in which Trump boasted: 'When you're a star . . . you can do anything . . . Grab 'em by the pussy. You can do anything.'

2 April 2023
Chris Riddell
Observer

The consumer launch of ChatGPT – an 'artificial intelligence chatbot', providing credibly human-type answers to online questions – focused attention on the latest advances in AI technology. On 22 March 2023, the Future of Life Institute, dedicated to steering 'transformative technologies away from extreme, large-scale risks and towards benefiting life', issued a warning note on AI by way of an open letter: 'Pause Giant AI Experiments'. Tesla founder Elon Musk and Apple's co-founder Steve Wozniak were just two of those who signed the letter, which asked worriedly: 'Should we develop nonhuman minds that might eventually outnumber, outsmart, obsolete [*sic*] and replace us?'

3 April 2023
Steve Bright
Sun

As the Easter holidays began, the port of Dover was once again beset by long delays and tailbacks for travellers trying to get to the continent. Exasperated coach parties told the *Metro* newspaper of 16-hour hold-ups and having to stay overnight in their seats, with no information; one coach driver told *Sky News* that the toilet facilities were 'harrowing'. Suella Braverman denied that the delays were 'an adverse effect of Brexit'. However, a Downing Street spokesman admitted that 'new processes' – involving the French authorities inspecting and stamping each British passport – were a contributing factor.

3 April 2023
Christian Adams
Evening Standard

THE OLD BALL 'N' CHAIN ...

7 April 2023
Dave Brown
Independent

On 5 April, Scottish police arrested Nicola Surgeon's husband, Peter Murrell, in connection with what they described as 'an ongoing investigation into the funding and finances of the Scottish National Party'. The couple's house was then cordoned off with police tape, and a lengthy search began, in the glare of the media. Murrell had been the party's chief executive until March. Sturgeon denied that her resignation as first minister had had anything to do with the investigation; she also denied any foreknowledge of 'Police Scotland's actions or intentions'. Murrell was released without charge on 7 April, but investigations continued.

Douglas Ross, leader of the Scottish Conservatives, gave a strong hint that the electorate should vote tactically, when he told the *Sunday Telegraph*: 'Where there is the strongest candidate to beat the SNP, you get behind that candidate.' This would mean Conservative voters switching, in many cases, to supporting Labour or Liberal Democrat candidates. Quickly, there was pushback from a Conservative spokesman, who insisted that Ross's remarks were 'emphatically not the view of the Conservative Party' – and soon Ross himself was rowing back on his words. Nevertheless, opponents were circling to the SNP, sensing an opportunity to capitalise on its current difficulties.

10 April 2023
Patrick Blower
Daily Telegraph

Do you think trying to appear as right wing as the Tories only makes you look a t**t?

KEIR STARMER DOESN'T.

Labour will NOT lock up dangerous clothes thieves!

12 April 2023
Dave Brown
Independent

An angry row erupted over a Labour 'attack advert', which showed a photograph of Rishi Sunak next to the words 'Do you think adults convicted of sexually assaulting children should go to prison? Rishi Sunak doesn't' – followed by the claim that 'Labour will lock up dangerous child abusers.' The advertisement was condemned by critics across the political spectrum, from Conservatives to Labour left-wingers like former shadow chancellor John McDonnell. Sir Keir Starmer, however, made 'absolutely zero apologies for being blunt' about the Conservative record on imprisonments for child abuse, as well as the 'thugs, gangs and monsters' who 'mock our justice system'.

President Biden landed at RAF Aldergrove, next to Belfast International Airport, for the start of a four-day visit to the island of Ireland, the land of his ancestors. A principal reason was to emphasise 'the US commitment to preserving peace': it was the 25th anniversary of the Good Friday Agreement, which had ended 30 years of the violent 'Troubles', and which Biden's predecessor President Clinton had helped to nurture. Rishi Sunak greeted Biden. At 5 feet 6 inches in height, Sunak was – according to *The Oldie* – the shortest male prime minister since Winston Churchill and 6 inches shorter than Biden.

13 April 2023
Steven Camley
Herald Scotland

17 April 2023
Nicola Jennings
Guardian

Documents leaked in March indicated the sheer scale of staffing problems in the NHS. They forecast that urgent action would be needed to avert a shortfall of tens of thousands of GPs, community nurses and paramedics in the coming 15 years. The documents suggested that the NHS currently lacked more than 150,000 staff necessary to make it function properly and effectively. In April, while health workers in the union Unison accepted a government pay offer of 5 per cent, members of the Royal College of Nursing rejected it – and announced new strike days.

On 13 April, the usual 'purdah' rules came into force, given that local elections in England were scheduled for 4 May. These rules effectively forbid the governing party from taking advantage of its position by making major policy announcements shortly before elections. However, on 17 April, Rishi Sunak made a speech in north London, elaborating on proposals for teenagers to study some maths to age 18; and the same day, Downing Street issued a press release entitled 'Prime Minister outlines his vision for Maths to 18'. A Liberal Democrat MP, Christine Jardine, asked the cabinet secretary to investigate a possible purdah breach.

18 April 2023
Patrick Blower
Daily Telegraph

Following his state visit to China, Emmanuel Macron ruffled transatlantic feathers by telling reporters that Europe should not follow 'an American rhythm' on Taiwan, lest it become a 'vassal'. Instead, he saw Europe as a 'third pole', distinct from the United States and China. According to the cartoonist, 'Of all the animals which symbolically represent countries, the Russian bear and the Chinese dragon are the most used and the most apt. Every time I do a cartoon about China, I tell myself to come up with a different image, to avoid the dragon cliché. Mostly these attempts end in failure. It just works too well.'

18 April 2023
Peter Schrank
The Times

With many consumers cutting back on their weekly shopping baskets, the Office of National Statistics confirmed that UK food-price inflation in the year to March 2023 had increased at the second-highest rate among the G7 countries, beaten only by Germany. And overall, food prices had risen 26 per cent since pre-Covid-19 days. In April, King Charles and Camilla, the Queen Consort, designated a 'deep quiche with a crisp, light pastry case and delicate flavours of spinach, broad beans and fresh tarragon' as 'Coronation Quiche': something the public might prepare, if they wished, as part of their own coronation celebrations.

20 April 2023
Ella Baron
The Times

..5..4..3..

We have rapid unscheduled disassembly

22 April 2023
Steven Camley
Herald Scotland

The political career of Dominic Raab appeared to detonate with the appearance of an official report into accusations that he had bullied civil servants. It found that he had sometimes acted in an 'intimidating way' and exhibited 'an abuse or misuse of power'. Within 24 hours, Raab had resigned, while nevertheless attacking the report as setting a 'dangerous precedent'. The day before, Elon Musk's SpaceX company test-launched Starship, the world's largest rocket. It soared upwards for four minutes before exploding, or, in the company's description, experiencing a 'rapid unscheduled disassembly'.

On 23 April, all UK devices equipped with 4G and 5G connectivity were meant to receive a 10-second official alert, including the message: 'This is a test of Emergency Alerts, a new UK government service that will warn you if there is a life-threatening emergency nearby.' At the same time, Labour's former shadow home secretary Diane Abbott became embroiled in an antisemitism row for implying, in the *Observer*, that Jewish people might suffer prejudice but not racism. Although Abbott quickly tried to disassociate herself from her own remarks, she lost the Labour whip, and an investigation into her conduct was set in motion.

24 April 2023
Christian Adams
Evening Standard

27 April 2023
Steve Bell
Guardian

Speaking on a podcast, the Bank of England's chief economist, Huw Pill, said that trying to beat inflation through wage rises could not work. Rather, people and companies needed 'to accept that they're worse off and stop trying to maintain their real spending power by bidding up prices, whether through higher wages or passing energy costs on to customers'. Meanwhile, the *Guardian* claimed to have made 'the first comprehensive audit' of King Charles's assets, putting them at more than £1.8 billion – over three times the king's wealth as calculated by the forthcoming *Sunday Times* Rich List for 2023. A key factor, asserted the *Guardian*, was exemption from inheritance tax.

Richard Sharp, the government-appointed chairman of the BBC, had been mired in a controversy for several months, after the *Sunday Times* revealed that before he got the job (in 2021) he had helped introduce a contact offering Boris Johnson a £800,000 personal loan guarantee. Now, the commissioner of public appointments concluded that there had been a 'potential perceived conflict of interest', since Johnson had approved Sharp's appointment, other candidates were sidelined, and Sharp – a former donor to the Conservative Party – had failed to mention the loan guarantee during his interview. Given that verdict, Sharp resigned.

29 April 2023
Peter Brookes
The Times

Bruised and battered, the Conservatives were haemorrhaging support ahead of forthcoming local English elections. Strategists seized on a 'worst case' study predicting a loss of 1,000 Conservative council seats, in the hope that anything better could be spun as a positive story. The elections would be the first to require voter identification at polling stations, as a result of the Elections Act 2022. Controversially, there seemed to be a wider array of officially acceptable ID for older voters, who disproportionately vote Conservative, leading to accusations of gerrymandering and potential disenfranchisement. Moreover, the evidence for voter fraud was small.

30 April 2023
Chris Riddell
Observer

As preparations were fine-tuned for King Charles's multi-million-pound coronation, a royally endorsed volunteering scheme – the Big Help Out – encouraged the British public to sign up for what the government called 'a cause they care about' on the Coronation Bank Holiday (8 May). For the cartoonist, the contrasts were stark: while Charles 'held on to his tax-free income, the taxpayer paid for his coronation. Meanwhile, nurses go to food banks to survive.'

1 May 2023
Nicola Jennings
Guardian

The archbishop of Canterbury, Justin Welby, asked members of the public to pledge their allegiance to King Charles III during his coronation. It was the first time in history that the public had been invited to participate in a 'homage of the people', replacing the traditional pledge from hereditary peers. Cardinal Vincent Nichols, the archbishop of Westminster, called it a 'lovely' and 'remarkable' moment. But Graham Smith, a spokesman for anti-monarchy group Republic, branded the gesture 'offensive' and 'tone deaf'. 'In a democracy it is the head of state who should be swearing allegiance to the people,' he commented, 'not the other way around.'

2 May 2023
Ian Knox
Belfast Telegraph

FIFTY SHADES OF SUE GRAY...

CABINET OFFICE REPORT

In March, Sue Gray – the civil servant who had investigated lockdown breaches at Downing Street – resigned to become Keir Starmer's chief of staff. Some Conservatives then suggested her Partygate report had not been objective, and the Cabinet Office launched an inquiry into when she had begun negotiations with Labour. Starmer insisted on both his and Gray's propriety and now accused the Cabinet Office of 'trying to resurrect' the story days before local elections. The bestselling erotic novels and films in the *Fifty Shades of Grey* series revolve around the sadomasochistic pains and pleasures of the world of its titular antihero, Christian Grey.

3 May 2023
Christian Adams
Evening Standard

On 3 May, two 'unmanned aerial vehicles' – drones – exploded above the Kremlin. The Russian authorities claimed that their defences had intercepted an attempted terrorist attack to kill Vladimir Putin, blaming Ukraine. Volodymyr Zelensky denied his country's involvement, saying 'We don't attack Putin, or Moscow' and insisting that Ukraine's war tactics were confined to defending its territory. Debate continued about whether the drones were operated from inside or outside Russia. Russian hardliners agitated for retaliation against Zelensky himself, but US Secretary of State Antony Blinken said that Washington had not been able to validate the reported attack, and that Russian assertions should be taken with a 'very large shaker of salt'.

4 May 2023
Patrick Blower
Daily Telegraph

Since King Charles's accession to the throne, republican protestors holding placards bearing the slogan 'Not My King' had become a familiar sight at the monarch's public appearances. Now, just days before the coronation, the Home Office's Police Powers Unit sent a letter to several campaign groups, including the anti-monarchist Republic, flagging up new restrictions on legal protest – and the penalties for breaching them. These had just come into force with the Police, Crime, Sentencing and Courts Act. Lawyers for Republic regarded the letters as 'intimidation'. The Metropolitan Police later expressed 'regret' for the unjustified arrest of six protestors on Coronation Day itself.

4 May 2023
Ben Jennings
Guardian

The Realm of Fantasy

According to the cartoonist, 'Rishi Sunak announced the UK's attempt to become a tech powerhouse to rival Silicon Valley . . . billboards were erected in San Francisco to entice American investors to Britain that read "Welcome to the Unicorn Kingdom". "Unicorn" was a term coined earlier this century for startup companies that have reached $1 billion . . . Like so many other post-Brexit pipe-dreams this initiative had the whiff of fantasy about it . . . In the UK we're pulling out all the fairy tale stops for the coronation of King Charles III in our own particular realm of fantasy.' King Charles III was crowned on 6 May at Westminster Abbey. The King and Queen Camilla left the ceremony in the historic Gold State Coach.

5 May 2023
Chris Duggan
The Times

CROWNED...

LOCAL ELECTIONS

DAVID SIMONDS 7.5.23

Local elections took place in England on 4 May, just two days before King Charles was crowned. Despite Conservative attempts to manage expectations, referring to predictions of a 1,000-seat loss (while anticipating a better outcome), the party's showing proved even worse. More than 1,060 Conservative council seats fell to other parties and to independents, with Labour, the Liberal Democrats and the Greens as chief beneficiaries. Conservatives were left controlling 33 councils, compared to 89 in 2019. Keir Starmer lauded the outcome as 'fantastic', while Rishi Sunak admitted that it was 'disappointing'.

7 May 2023
David Simonds
Evening Standard

In the English local elections, Labour gained more than 500 new councillors (and 22 councils), while the Liberal Democrats earned more than 400 new councillors (and took control of 12 more councils). In the heady victory atmosphere, though, there remained doubt as to whether those results put Labour on course for an absolute majority at the next general election – and therefore speculation about whether the Labour and Liberal Democrat leaders were discussing possible collaboration in power. Journalists noted that neither Keir Starmer nor Ed Davey would be drawn, while the BBC thought it looked like 'symmetrical flirting'.

7 May 2023
Steve Bright
Sun

Vladimir Putin and the Kremlin were mocked after only a single 83-year-old T-34 tank was present for the Victory Day parade. The annual event usually sees thousands of Russian soldiers march through Red Square accompanied by hundreds of military vehicles. This year's event was the smallest since 2008, with only around 8,000 troops (allegedly cadets and students, not military staff), just 125 pieces of equipment and no aircraft. It was thought that Russia had lost significant numbers of modern tanks in Ukraine and had attempted to plug the shortfall by taking Cold War-era models out of storage.

10 May 2023
Ian Knox
Belfast Telegraph

11 May 2023
Christian Adams
Evening Standard

Speaking in the House of Lords, Justin Welby, the Archbishop of Canterbury, launched a comprehensive attack on the government's Illegal Migration Bill, including the provision removing migrants to Rwanda that was so enthusiastically backed by Suella Braverman. He thought the bill 'utterly fails to take a long term and strategic view of the challenges of migration and undermines international cooperation'. Furthermore, he pronounced it 'isolationist': it was, he insisted, 'morally unacceptable and politically impractical to let the poorest countries deal with the crisis alone and cut our international aid'.

In the cartoonist's view, Keir Starmer was now 'rapidly backtracking on the ten pledges that he had made to Labour supporters while running for the leadership in 2020 – abolishing tuition fees, bringing public utilities into public ownership, reforming universal credit and increasing income tax for the top 5 per cent – vowing to "unite the party". He now stated that Labour was "likely to move on [from these commitments]". Far from uniting his party, it led many Labour supporters to question whether he ever meant what he originally said.' The cartoonist wondered: 'What does he actually stand for?'

12 May 2023
Andy Davey
Jewish Chronicle

Rishi Sunak and his cigar-loving secretary for environment, food and rural affairs, Thérèse Coffey, hosted a summit at Downing Street under the title 'Farm to Fork'. Here, politicians, food industry professionals and farming representatives considered the challenges to the UK's food supply chain against a background of farmers' dissatisfaction with post-Brexit arrangements and their forebodings about controversial trade deals Liz Truss had negotiated. The cartoon references the film *Withnail and I* (1987) in which two hapless Londoners go 'on holiday by mistake' to the Lake District before realising they are not cut out for country living.

17 May 2023
Dave Brown
Independent

In an interview with the BBC's *Newsnight*, Nigel Farage responded to critiques of Brexit outcomes by acknowledging that 'Brexit has failed'. He blamed over-regulation of business and government mishandling of the withdrawal process and its aftermath. 'We've not delivered on borders, we've not delivered on Brexit,' he claimed, because 'our politicians are about as useless as the commissioners in Brussels'. The phrase 'Does a bear shit in the woods?' is, according to the *Cambridge Dictionary*, 'a rude phrase used to say that the answer to a question you have just been asked is obviously "yes"'.

17 May 2023
Christian Adams
Evening Standard

19 May 2023
David Simonds
Evening Standard

The chief executive of the UK's biggest provider of broadband and mobile communications, BT Group, announced that his company was looking forward to 'a brighter future'. It would also, he said, mean 'a leaner business'. The effect of completing the installation of a fibre network, combined with advances in artificial intelligence, would mean more automation and a slimmed-down workforce – and save hundreds of millions of pounds in operating costs. According to the company's predictions, staffing could shrink by as much as 40 per cent, down to 75,000 by the end of the 2020s.

For the first time, the head of the water industry's trade body – Water UK – apologised in the media for the water companies' 'overspills of untreated sewage onto beaches and into rivers over the past few years'. She then went on to announce £10 billion of planned investment in water infrastructure, initially to be raised from investors but then to be clawed back through rising water bills in future years. While the water regulator said it would monitor progress and potential impacts on consumers, critics pointed to the fact that the sum of £10 billion was dwarfed by dividends paid out by water companies since their privatisation in 1989.

21 May 2023
Chris Riddell
Observer

TICK...TICK...TICK...

27 May 2023
Dave Brown
Independent

More controversies relating to Boris Johnson's premiership threatened to explode on Rishi Sunak's watch. Cabinet Office officials felt obliged to flag up sections of Johnson's official diaries to the police, which referred to visits made by Johnson's family and friends to the prime-ministerial country retreat at Chequers while the country was in lockdown. Johnson quickly rubbished claims of any rule breaking. At the same time, the official Covid-19 Inquiry, under Lady Hallett, was demanding Johnson's unredacted WhatsApp messages – a request, in this case, opposed by the Cabinet Office. The cartoon pays homage to one of artist Clive Upton's best-known illustrations, *Bomb Disposal: Listening for Ticking* (1942).

On the afternoon of 25 May, the driver of a silver Kia crashed his car into the gates of Downing Street, prompting newsflashes and alarm about a possible terrorist incident. Police arrested the 43-year-old driver for criminal damage but released him two days later, pending a court appearance on an unrelated charge. Just days before, it was alleged that Suella Braverman had asked civil servants to arrange a private speed-awareness course for her – until told it was an inappropriate request. Braverman insisted she had instead paid her speeding fine and earned points on her licence, but pressure mounted on Sunak to investigate a possible breach of the Ministerial Code.

27 May 2023
Ben Jennings
Guardian

Flush...

Recep Tayyip Erdogan completed a flush of election victories on 28 May, after Turkish voters put him at their country's helm yet again, continuing his two-decade dominance of Turkish politics. Erdogan, often described as 'authoritarian', had recently distanced Turkey from its NATO partners' support for Ukraine, preferring a role as a potential broker between Russia and Ukraine. It was no wonder that Vladimir Putin, in wooing mode, congratulated his 'dear friend', asserted that Erdogan's latest victory was the result of the president's 'selfless work', and applauded Turkey's 'independent foreign policy'.

30 May 2023
Seamus Jennings
The Times

According to the cartoonist, this cartoon was 'based around Chancellor Jeremy Hunt's comments saying he was "comfortable" with a recession if it drove inflation down. The drawing demonstrates that while the wealthy leaders Hunt and Sunak can live through a recession, it's going to make an already hard situation so much worse for many in Britain. I really enjoyed making Rishi's mansion very over-the-top. The job listing for ex-chancellors reflects how this current government feels like its members are eyeing up more lucrative jobs down the line.' He added: 'I got a number of comments saying the pool I drew for Rishi is way smaller than the real thing.'

31 May 2023
Tom Johnston
Guardian

2 June 2023
Ben Jennings
Guardian

On 1 June the Cabinet Office applied for a judicial review into whether it had to hand over Boris Johnson's unredacted WhatsApp messages and diaries to the official Covid-19 Inquiry. The government's argument was that the totality of the records would contain much that was irrelevant; but the attempt to conceal them encouraged speculation that the government was keen to suppress potentially embarrassing revelations. The next day, in an unusual move, Johnson announced that he wanted to hand over the material and requested that the Cabinet Office pass along his old notebooks to the inquiry. The move was widely seen a swipe at Rishi Sunak's government.

In late May, senior Labour politicians criticised Britain's over-reliance on cheap overseas workers. Shadow Home Secretary Yvette Cooper told journalists that Labour would look at time-limited visas for foreign workers in 'shortage occupations' as a way to pressurise British firms into training up more UK citizens. Labour also announced that it would do away with rules permitting companies to pay overseas workers 20 per cent less than their UK counterparts. Meanwhile, the government launched an advertising campaign to deter Albanian nationals from crossing the Channel 'illegally'. It appeared that both parties were keen to burnish their credentials of being tough on migrants.

2 June 2023
Dave Brown
Independent

Back in 2010, Prime Minister David Cameron had promised to reduce net migration to 'tens of thousands' each year. In May 2023, Rishi Sunak insisted he would reduce migration below the levels he had inherited. But the latest official statistics, to June 2022, showed a continued rise in long-term net migration to 606,000, mostly non-EU, with the numbers swelled by those arriving on 'protection routes' from Ukraine and Hong Kong. On 26 May, the presenter Philip Schofield resigned from ITV and his longstanding slot as co-anchor of *This Morning*, admitting an 'unwise but not illegal' affair with a much younger male colleague.

5 June 2023
Christian Adams
Evening Standard

As sporting bodies continued to ban female transgender athletes from competing in women's categories, both the Liberal Democrat and Labour leaders found themselves quizzed on gender issues. Ed Davey, distinguishing biological sex from gender, told LBC radio host Nick Ferrari that while the 'vast majority' of people with female biological sex 'feel they're women', there was 'a very small number who don't feel like that'. When asked whether a woman could have a penis, he therefore acknowledged: 'Well, quite clearly.' Sir Keir Starmer had previously spoken in similar terms, suggesting that 99.9 per cent – but therefore not 100 per cent – of women lacked a penis.

5 June 2023
Steve Bright
Sun

7 June 2023
Patrick Blower
Daily Telegraph

Early on 6 June, the Ukrainian Kakhovka dam collapsed, sending damaging flood waters over a wide area along the Dnieper (Dnipro) River down to the city of Kherson, and affecting both Ukrainian-held territory and Russian-occupied land. The timing coincided with the beginnings of Ukraine's long-awaited counter-offensive. President Zelensky immediately called the dam's destruction an act of Russian terrorism, and investigators subsequently alleged Russian explosives were involved. But Vladimir Putin declared it a Ukrainian war crime. The UK said it was too early to establish the facts. As the reservoir dried up, so did the canals supplying southern Ukraine with water.

On 6 June, the Duke of Sussex became the first senior royal figure since Victoria's son Prince Albert – the future King Edward VII – to give evidence in a public court. Prince Harry was a witness in the case against Mirror Group Newspapers, alleging it had obtained private information illegally between the 1990s and 2011. Over two days, the prince spent eight hours in the witness box. The relative term 'my truth', as opposed to 'the truth', was used by the Duchess of Sussex during a 2021 interview with Oprah Winfrey.

7 June 2023
Ella Baron
Guardian

11 June 2023
Chris Riddell
Observer

Donald Trump achieved a historical milestone on 14 June by becoming the first US ex-president to be charged with federal crimes. The 37 counts, when they were unsealed, related to withholding confidential defence records after his time in office, sharing some of them with others, and obstructing official efforts to retrieve them. During the 2016 presidential race, Trump had goaded his supporters into chanting 'Lock her up!', in reference to his Democratic rival Hillary Clinton's use of a private email server for some confidential information when she was secretary of state. Although Clinton was found to have been careless, the FBI had found no grounds for prosecution.

On 9 June, Boris Johnson issued a blistering statement announcing his resignation as an MP. He had seen the results of the Privileges Committee's investigation into whether he had misled Parliament over Partygate. Now, he attacked the committee's procedures as a 'witch-hunt' that was attempting to 'drive me out' and accused its chair of 'egregious bias'. The committee's report was not yet public, but if the House were to uphold any recommendation for a ten-day (or more) suspension of Johnson, it would likely result in a recall petition – and pave the way for a by-election. In the words of the BBC, 'He decided to jump before he was pushed.'

12 June 2023
Nicola Jennings
Guardian

13 June 2023
Henny Beaumont
Guardian

Tensions between Rishi Sunak and Boris Johnson erupted over the former prime minister's resignation honours list. The House of Lords Appointments Commission (HOLAC) had removed eight names from the list during its vetting procedures, including four sitting MPs. Sunak claimed that Johnson had then wanted him to overrule the commission and reinstate the names – which Sunak said he was 'not prepared to do'. Johnson disputed this version of events, claiming that Sunak was 'talking rubbish'. As the *Guardian* described it, in this cartoon 'the Tory Party is burnt out', while 'Fireman Rishi' tries to put out the fires that 'Boris Johnson keeps stoking'.

Silvio Berlusconi, the most colourful Italian politician of modern times, died on 12 June, aged eighty-six. He had made several political comebacks to serve as Italy's prime minister longer than anyone else in living memory, leading four governments between 1994 and 2011. But the media tycoon was equally well known for his many scandals, from *bunga-bunga* sex parties to charges (and convictions) for corruption and bribery. His ability to bounce back from controversies that would sink others seemed to be the aspiration for many politicians of later decades.

13 June 2023
Steven Camley
Herald Scotland

16 June 2023
Graeme Bandeira
Northern Agenda

Boris Johnson's resignation as an MP had been preceded by a declaration from his close ally Nadine Dorries that she would stand down 'with immediate effect'. Writing in the *Daily Mail*, she made plain her fury at the fact that she would not, after all, be receiving a peerage, which she regarded as a personal snub from Rishi Sunak's 'posh boys'. Nigel Adams – another Johnson supporter omitted from the post-vetting resignation honours list – also announced he would stand down. Yet, by the time that Parliament went into summer recess, Dorries had still not actually resigned.

BYE BYE BORIS

WORLD KING

DISHONOURS LIST
SIR HAUNTED PENCIL ✓
BARONESS INTERN ✓

BARONESS KANGAROO ANUS ✗

RIDDELL
18.6.23

Despite the arguments about names allegedly 'blocked' from Boris Johnson's resignation honours list, the remaining 40-plus names were enough to generate heated controversies of their own and attract accusations that Johnson was rewarding fellow Partygate miscreants and bringing the sytem into disrepute. A Conservative aide told Sky News it represented 'rewards for failure', while an ex-cabinet minister summed it up as 'put out the trash day' (according to the *Guardian*). There was renewed criticism of Sunak for not blocking or amending the list, though that would have created an precedent for future honours lists.

18 June 2023
Chris Riddell
Observer

TORY CHICKEN RUN AFTER AARDMAN

20 June 2023
Ella Baron
Guardian

On 19 June, the House of Commons debated the Privileges Committee report on Boris Johnson, which asserted that he had committed 'repeated contempts of Parliament'. Had Johnson not resigned, its recommended sanction would have been a 90-day suspension from Parliament. In the event, Labour forced a successful resolution to approve the report. Just six Conservatives voted against, but many abstained, including Michael Gove, and others were absent, including Rishi Sunak, who pleaded other engagements. Welsh First Minister Mark Drakeford described Sunak's non-appearance as 'an astonishing act of political cowardice'. The cartoon references *Chicken Run* (2000), a Aardman animation film.

Newspapers picked up a story that during a 'life education' class at Rye College, East Sussex, a girl apparently wished to identify as a cat. A fellow pupil said she was 'genuinely unwell – crazy'. The teacher admonished that pupil for calling her classmate crazy, before a heated discussion (caught on audio recording) ensued on the subject of biological sex versus gender. Two pupils insisted gender meant just girls and boys, while the teacher, asserting that there were many genders, said she would be reporting the pupils to senior staff and added: 'You need to have a proper educational conversation about equality, diversity and inclusion.'

22 June 2023
Patrick Blower
Daily Telegraph

On 22 June, the Bank of England raised interest rates to 5 per cent – the highest rate in 15 years – inevitably bringing higher mortgage payments for thousands of people. Three days later, in an interview with the BBC's Laura Kuenssberg, Rishi Sunak insisted that 'inflation is the enemy' and asked the British people to 'be reassured that we've got to hold our nerve, stick to the plan'. Criticism ensued – of the Bank for doing too little too late, and Sunak for offering platitudes rather than financial help. The animated film *Up* (2009), made by Pixar, features a house raised higher and higher by a multitude of balloons.

24 June 2023
Seamus Jennings
Guardian

For a few days in June, the world was gripped by news of mutiny among Russia's fighting forces and the possibility of civil war, even a coup, in Russia. As the cartoonist put it, 'A defining moment in Russia's war in Ukraine and potentially a challenge to Putin's grip on power was when [Yevgeny] Prigozhin's Wagner [mercenary] troops embarked on an armed rebellion. Putin called it "a stab in the back of our country". Wagner forces crossed from Ukraine into Rostov-on-Don without opposition. Prigozhin's hubris was a taunt to his erstwhile master – the man who created the beast: Putin.'

25 June 2023
Andy Davey
Sunday Telegraph

27 June 2023
Christian Adams
Evening Standard

As the last Indiana Jones film – *Dial of Destiny* – prepared for cinema release, Matt Hancock had his own date with destiny when he appeared before the Covid-19 Inquiry. Hancock had been health secretary before the pandemic and for much of its course. Now, he accepted 'responsibility for all the things that happened' in his department and apologised for 'each death'. In his view, major errors in pre-pandemic thinking had been the assumptions that a pandemic would be a type of influenza, and that it would be unstoppable, so that the emphasis had been too much on reacting to a disaster rather than trying to prevent it.

The sudden resignation of Sarah Bentley as chief executive of Thames Water was the prelude to a crisis at Britain's largest provider of water and sewerage services. With revelations that the company, which served 15 million customers, was saddled with £14 billion of debt, the government moved to prepare contingency plans for a taxpayer rescue via 'special administration' should its pension-fund and sovereign-wealth-fund investors not stump up. Thames Water had declared a pre-tax profit of more than £1 billion in 2022 and paid its (now) ex-CEO £1.5 million in 2022–23. Yet leaks in its region had reached a five-year high and sewage discharges into waterways continued.

29 June 2023
Dave Brown
Independent

Having dealt with Boris Johnson, the Parliamentary Privileges Committee turned their attention to several Johnson-supporting MPs and peers who, in their view, had attempted to 'impugn the integrity of the committee'. Prominent among the ten individuals named were Nadine Dorries and Sir Jacob Rees-Mogg – his knighthood a result of Johnson's resignation honours – who had used their media platforms on TalkTV and GB News for 'the most vociferous attacks' or to 'lobby or intimidate' committee members. On 28 June, during the first Ashes Test at Lord's, the England wicket keeper Jonny Bairstow carried a Just Stop Oil protestor off the pitch to the boundary line.

29 June 2023
Christian Adams
Evening Standard

A fresh wave of protests took place across France after a police officer shot and killed a 17-year-old delivery driver of North African descent following a chase. According to the cartoonist, 'Hundreds of rioters are arrested as clashes between police and protestors in France continue for a third night. Shops ransacked, cars set on fire, and yet people still use cafes "comme d'habitude" even as fires break out in neighbouring buildings.' French President Emmanuel Macron 'strongly condemn[ed] all of those who are using this situation and this moment to try and create disorder'.

1 July 2023
Andy Davey
Telegraph

FREE CASH WITHDRAWALS

IN ORDER TO PROCEED, PLEASE DECLARE ANY CONTROVERSIAL OPINIONS

Blower 4.7.23

At the end of June Nigel Farage took to Twitter to claim that his bank – later confirmed to be Coutts – had cancelled his accounts without explanation. On 4 July, the BBC reported that the decision had been taken due to lack of funds (Coutts requires that clients hold at least £1 million in investments or £3 million in savings). However, later in the month, the former UKIP leader published a document that revealed Coutts had cancelled the accounts due to the 'significant reputational risks of being associated with him'. The BBC apologised to Farage for their inaccurate reporting, and Alison Rose, chief executive officer of Coutts' owner NatWest, resigned after admitting to being the source of the false report.

4 July 2023
Patrick Blower
Telegraph

A group of Conservative MPs who called themselves the New Conservatives urged the prime minister to drastically cut migration. Recently released figures from the Office for National Statistics showed that the UK's population had grown by 600,000 in the last year. The New Conservatives' suggestion was to cancel a scheme that grants work visas to care workers. At the same time, the Skills for Care charity warned that the number of vacancies in social care was at the highest ever, with 165,000 unfilled posts in 2021–22. Meanwhile, three members of the Marylebone Cricket Club were suspended after clashes with the Australian team in the Long Room of the club during the second test of the Ashes.

4 July 2023
Morten Morland
The Times

Thirty million users signed up in the first day to Meta's new social media app, Threads, according to the company's CEO, Mark Zuckerberg. The app was billed as a 'friendly' rival to Twitter and experts predicted that Threads would attract users who are unhappy with many of the changes made to Twitter (later rebranded as X) following Elon Musk's takeover in October 2022. In June, Zuckerberg and Musk had agreed to fight each other in a cage match. In other news, the latest instalment in the Mission: Impossible franchise, *Dead Reckoning Part One*, opened at cinemas nationwide.

6 July 2023
David Simonds
Evening Standard

Labour leader Sir Keir Starmer announced his party's plans to reform the education system – but his speech was drowned out by climate protestors. According to the cartoonist, 'Starmer unrolls his Big New Idea – which, like all Starmer's recent policy announcements, follows Sunak's gambits like a bad smell. His "Five Missions" is a carbon copy of Sunak's "Five Pledges" with the words rearranged. It is interrupted by the ubiquitous Just Stop Oil protestors.' The climate activists heckled Starmer for watering down his previous commitment to spend £28 billion on a green prosperity plan – a U-turn that Labour blamed on rising interest rates.

7 July 2023
Andy Davey
Telegraph

7 July 2023
Graeme Bandeira
Northern Agenda

On 5 July, the country marked 75 years of the National Health Service. The anniversary, however, was marred by warnings that the institution may not make it to 100. In June hospital waiting lists in England had reached a record high of 7.4 million. Tens of thousands of cancer patients faced life-threatening delays. Health leaders said the cause of the problems was staffing shortages, with 112,000 staff vacancies unfilled, including 43,000 nurses. New strikes among junior doctors and hospital consultants were also expected.

Minister of State for Immigration Robert Jenrick ordered that murals of Mickey Mouse and other cartoon characters be removed from the walls of a centre for unaccompanied child migrants. The murals had been designed to welcome child asylum seekers, but reports suggested that Jenrick felt the images were too friendly. Sources told the *i* newspaper that staff were 'horrified' by the 'cruel' order. Labour's shadow immigration minister, Stephen Kinnock, said that the approach indicated a 'chaotic government in crisis, whose failing approach means all they have left is tough talk and cruel and callous policies'.

8 July 2023
Ben Jennings
Guardian

LIVE

BBC

BBC NEWS
BREAKING

12 July 2023
Morten Morland
The Times

On 7 July, the *Sun* reported that a top BBC presenter had been accused of paying a teenager for sexually explicit photos. On 11 July, BBC News reported that the same presenter had sent threatening messages to another young person. The speculation around the presenter's identity became so fierce that many TV personalities took to social media to deny their involvement and to call on the accused presenter to identify themselves. The following day Vicky Flind, wife of newsreader Huw Edwards, revealed that her husband was the presenter at the centre of the allegations. Meanwhile, the NATO summit took place in Lithuania, with G7 members agreeing a security pact with Ukraine.

Keir Starmer announced that he would keep the two-child benefit cap if Labour were to win the next general election, despite having opposed the cap when campaigning to be party leader. The cap, which prevents parents from claiming child tax credit or universal credit for any third or subsequent child born after April 2017, was introduced by former Conservative chancellor George Osborne. This U-turn generated backlash from some Labour MPs who worried that Labour's promises are not different enough from the Conservatives going into the next election. The quiz show *University Challenge* returned to screens on 17 July with new host Amol Rajan.

18 July 2023
Christian Adams
Evening Standard

The Conservatives narrowly held on to their seat in Boris Johnson's old constituency of Uxbridge and South Ruislip but suffered two heavy defeats in a night of three dramatic by-elections. In Somerton and Frome the Liberal Democrats took the seat by overturning a majority of 19,000 votes, and Labour made history by overturning a 20,137 majority in Selby and Ainsty. According to the cartoonist, 'Sunak insisted his Tories are still in the game after marginally retaining the Uxbridge seat . . . There is a "glimmer of hope" apparently . . . The polls suggest he was mistaken – the Tories are 20 points behind, nationally. Whether or not the good ship Tory goes down, his future looks uncertain.'

23 July 2023
Andy Davey
Telegraph

Keir Starmer held talks with Sadiq Khan after blaming the London mayor's Ultra-Low Emissions Zone (ULEZ) for Labour's narrow defeat in the Uxbridge by-election. ULEZ, which involves a daily charge for all vehicles that don't meet emissions standards, had previously only applied to more central areas of London, but Khan's proposal was to extend the policy to all London boroughs. Starmer said that there was 'no doubt' that the scheme cost the party the by-election (by only 495 votes) and called for 'reflection' on how the expansion would be carried out.

24 July 2023
Patrick Blower
Telegraph

There were tensions in the Conservative Party over climate policies after Housing Secretary Michael Gove said some of the government's initiatives should be reviewed but that the 2030 ban on new petrol and diesel car sales was 'immovable'. Rishi Sunak had announced that he remained committed to achieving a net zero by 2050 but that any new climate measures would have to be 'proportionate and pragmatic' and not 'unnecessarily' add 'hassle'. The prime minister was facing calls to row back on some of his green policies following the response to ULEZ in the Uxbridge by-election.

26 July 2023
Peter Schrank
The Times

Only hours after being discharged from hospital following an emergency heart procedure, Benjamin Netanyahu led his coalition government in passing controversial legislation to overhaul Israel's supreme court. The bill limits the supreme court's ability to overturn government decisions and gives politicians more control over judicial appointments. Critics claim that the bill undermines Israel's democracy, while right-wing politicians allege that the court is too powerful. Police used water cannon and skunk gas to disperse the crowds after approximately 20,000 protestors surrounded the parliament building. Bell's cartoon references *Expulsion from the Garden of Eden* by Masaccio.

26 July 2023
Steve Bell
Guardian

Seeking to replenish its forces on the frontline in Ukraine, the Russian parliament voted to raise the maximum age of conscripts from 27 to 30. The law increases the number of recruits eligible for a year of compulsory service and also prevents conscripts from leaving the country once they have received their draft notice. In September 2022 thousands of men fled Russia after President Putin announced a mobilisation of 300,000 reservists to support forces in Ukraine. The task of conscripting combat personnel had become more difficult due to undisclosed casualties in Ukraine.

26 July 2023
Patrick Blower
Telegraph

The UN secretary general, António Guterres, said that the era of global warming had ended and the 'era of global boiling has arrived', after scientists announced that July was set to be the hottest month on record. The effects of the extreme heat were seen across the world: thousands of tourists fled wildfires in Greece and many more endured extreme heat waves across the United States and China. According to Lord Frost, however, the rising temperatures were 'likely to be beneficial' to the UK, as it meant fewer people would die due to cold winters. The former Conservative minister and Brexit negotiator also said he was 'sceptical' about green policies to mitigate climate change.

30 July 2023
Chris Riddell
Observer

Number 10 revealed that the government was planning to award 100-plus new drilling licences to maximise the oil and gas being extracted from the North Sea. Rishi Sunak said that the plan was 'entirely consistent with our plan to get to net zero' as domestic supplies were significantly more efficient than shipping gas from abroad, but many climate activists challenged his claims. Mike Childs, head of policy for Friends of the Earth, said: 'Climate change is already battering the planet . . . granting hundreds of new oil and gas licences will simply pour more fuel on the flames, while doing nothing for energy security.'

31 July 2023
Christian Adams
Evening Standard

Critics slammed Rishi Sunak's 'helicopter lifestyle' after it was revealed that he borrowed a Conservative donor's luxury helicopter to travel 200 miles, on a journey that would have taken only 10 minutes longer by train. The journey would have emitted more than a tonne of CO_2 into the atmosphere in the hottest month yet recorded. Meanwhile, train passengers faced continued disruption as 20,000 rail workers in the RMT union walked out in a dispute over pay and job security. Negotiations with the government had been going on for more than a year without a resolution.

31 July 2023
Nicola Jennings
Guardian

The Bank of England raised interest rates from 5 to 5.25 per cent – its 14th consecutive rise – as inflation remained stubbornly high. The governor of the Bank of England, Andrew Bailey, said that rates had to be raised because 'we've got to get inflation back down to target.' Chancellor Jeremy Hunt recognised that the hike constituted 'a lot of pain for families'. According to the cartoonist, 'This was uncharted territory for Captain Sunak and his sidekick Hunt. It's not clear they knew what they were doing or where they were headed. Ditto Engineer Bailey, whose only option is to keep raising the warp speed without much of an effect.'

4 August 2023
Andy Davey
Telegraph

On 4 August, Donald Trump appeared in court in Washington to plead not guilty to trying to overturn the results of the 2020 election. These charges constituted the third criminal case being brought against Trump: he also faced charges in New York related to falsifying business records and 40 felony counts in Florida for illegally retaining classified documents. Trump said that 'this is a persecution of a person that is leading by very, very substantial numbers in the Republican primary.' Opinion polls showed that Republican support for Trump had surged since the first indictment in March – he was now leading the second-place candidate, Ron DeSantis, by 30 percentage points.

6 August 2023
Chris Riddell
Observer

A Home Office minister confirmed that the government was considering sending refugees to Ascension Island, a small volcanic island 4,000 miles from the UK. The government had been forced to change tack after the Court of Appeal ruled in late June that it was unlawful to send asylum seekers to Rwanda. Minister Sarah Dines said that, while the government was 'pretty confident that Rwanda is a legal policy', the government was now '[looking] at additional methods'. Meanwhile, the UK's biggest water firms were facing legal action for allegedly under-reporting the amount of raw sewage being pumped into rivers and seas. Storm Antoni was also bringing 'unseasonably strong' winds and heavy rain.

8 August 2023
Ben Jennings
Guardian

It was reported that at least two people had turned down honours nominations from former prime minister Liz Truss. One allegedly said that it would be too 'humiliating' to accept the honour from the UK's shortest-serving prime minister, while the other said that they did not deserve it. Truss, who spent only 49 days in office, had nominated four people for life peerages and twelve for honours – which equated to an honour for every three and half days of her premiership.

8 August 2023
Morten Morland
The Times

Back in April, the government confirmed that it intended to house up to 500 male migrants on an accommodation barge to cut the £6 million per day cost of housing them in hotels. The scheme was repeatedly delayed, including after firefighters warned that the barge was a 'potential death trap'. On 9 August, the Conservative Party deputy chairman, Lee Anderson, commented that asylum seekers who didn't want to be housed on the barge should 'fuck off back to France'. Justice Secretary Alex Chalk defended Anderson, saying he was merely articulating the 'righteous indignation of the British people'.

10 August 2023
Steve Bell
Guardian

Nadine Dorries was facing calls to immediately resign her seat in Parliament due to 'absenteeism'. The MP for Mid Bedfordshire had announced she intended to stand down in June, but later said she would not resign before receiving information on why she had been denied a peerage. According to records, Dorries had not spoken in the Commons since July 2022 and had voted on legislation on only four days in the past year, most recently in April. MPs earn a basic salary of £86,580 for not participating in the Commons. In July, Flitwick Town Council in Mid Bedfordshire urged Dorries to 'immediately vacate' the seat, noting that she had not held a surgery in the town since March 2020.

11 August 2023
Graeme Bandeira
Northern Agenda

Junior doctors began a four-day strike, the fifth this year, in a dispute over pay and deteriorating working conditions. Over 830,000 hospital appointments had to be cancelled. According to the cartoonist, 'I would have preferred this cartoon to be less even-handed. The finger of blame pointing more at the government. But this was for *The Times*. I was standing in for Peter Brookes and didn't want to stick my neck out (I suspect he would have done). I couldn't resist the link to the Crooked House fire and subsequent demolition.' The Crooked House near Dudley, once known as 'Britain's wonkiest pub', was demolished two days after a fire destroyed the building.

12 August 2023
Peter Schrank
The Times

The first migrants were moved onboard the *Bibby Stockholm* (the accommodation barge designed to house asylum seekers) on 7 August, but then had to be evacuated three days later after *Legionella* bacteria were found in the water system. Residents were offered a health check and moved back to government hotels, adding to the already significant cost. Rishi Sunak returned from holiday to find that NHS waiting lists had reached a new high (up to 7.6 million), junior doctors were on strike, and a National Institute of Economic and Social Research report had been published that found that 1.2 million families will run out of savings in the next year because of soaring mortgage repayments.

14 August 2023
David Simonds
Evening Standard

18 August 2023
Rob Murray
Daily Telegraph

New figures from the Office for National Statistics (ONS) found that inflation had slowed to 6.8 per cent in the year to July, due to lower energy costs. However, the ONS warned that food still cost 15 per cent more than one year previously and inflation remained three times higher than the Bank of England's 2 per cent target. A-level results were also released on 17 August. The proportion of A and A* grades fell sharply – by 9 percentage points – as exam boards opted to revert to pre-pandemic grading after two years of teacher-based assessment.

Donald Trump was arrested for the fourth time in five months. The former president surrendered himself to the court in Georgia – where he faces 13 charges of conspiring to overturn the results of the 2020 election – before being released on bail. Trump also had his mugshot taken, which is a first for a former US president. Yevgeny Prigozhin, who had led the Wagner group in a mutiny against Russian forces in June, was on the passenger list of a plane that crashed in Russia, killing all on board. Frenzied speculation about the cause of the crash ensued, with many suggesting that President Putin had motive for revenge. Putin later described Prigozhin as a 'talented man' who 'made serious mistakes'.

25 August 2023
Christian Adams
Evening Standard

Earlier in the month, the British Museum revealed that a member of staff had been sacked and the police were investigating after items of gold, jewellery and precious stones were reported missing. On 26 August, it was revealed that 2,000 items were unaccounted for and that the museum's director, Hartwig Fischer, was to step down. Meanwhile, President Putin signed a decree forcing all members of the Wagner group to swear an oath of allegiance to the Russian state. Analysts suggested that the move was an attempt to reassert authority over the private military group in the wake of Yevgeny Prigozhin's death.

27 August 2023
Rob Murray
Telegraph

Nadine Dorries officially resigned as an MP, more than two months after pledging to stand down 'with immediate effect'. Dorries launched a blistering attack against Rishi Sunak in her resignation letter, accusing him of running a 'zombie Parliament' and of flashing his 'gleaming smile', 'Prada shoes and Savile Row suits' instead of boosting opportunities. Dorries had come under pressure to resign for failing to participate in the Commons, despite earning over £86,000 for her work as an MP. Having written a series of novels, Dorries' latest book on the downfall of Boris Johnson was due to be published in September.

28 August 2023
Ella Baron
The Times

31 August 2023
Steve Bell
Guardian

The Ultra Low Emissions Zone (ULEZ) was expanded on 29 August, doubling in size to cover all London boroughs. The Labour mayor of London, Sadiq Khan, said it was a 'landmark' moment and that 'five million more Londoners will be breathing clean air.' But the expansion – which was first proposed by Boris Johnson – was met with fierce opposition, with demonstrators gathering outside Downing Street. Critics say that ULEZ will hit people on low incomes who cannot afford to replace their car. Earlier in the summer, Keir Starmer blamed the scheme for Labour's loss in the Uxbridge by-election. Rishi Sunak said that 'the mayor and Keir Starmer should explain to people why they think this is the right priority.'